FAMILY

Hope and Healing

MATTERS

Kwame Ronnie Vanderhorst

Copyright © 1997 by Prepare Our Youth, Inc.
All rights reserved. Published in the United States
of America by Hotep Productions, Washington, D.C.
Printed in U.S.A.
•

Typestyles Times Roman and AGaramond Semibold
No part of this book may be reproduced without
written permission from Prepare Our Youth and
Hotep Productions, except brief quotations for
critical articles and reviews.
•
ISBN 0-9652104-2-1

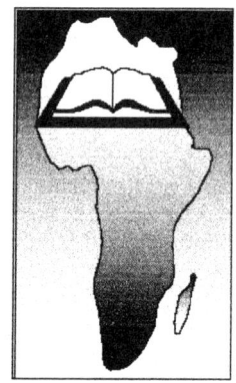

HOTEP PRODUCTIONS
© 1997

DEDICATED

TO JOHN & AMELIA PATTERSON,
MY WIFE'S PARENTS

YOU HAVE SHOWN ME THROUGH YOUR
LOVE AND ACCEPTANCE THAT FAMILY
MATTERS.
•
AND TO ALL FAMILIES
WHO NEED HOPE AND HEALING

ASANTE SANA

Onyamee Kwame, The Creator

•

My brother Steve, You pulled it off again!

•

Jomo Howard Bullard, You still "tha man!"

•

Carlton Davis, manuscript editor

•

Neva Brooks, for your never-ending support

•

Anthony "Tony" Adams, a genius ahead of his time

•

Maizyah R. McGhie, for your love of the truth

•

Baba Ted Adams, my mentor and friend

•

All the supporters of Prepare Our Youth

CONTENTS

Introduction > 6
Family Matters > 8
In The House > 17
Parenthood > 30
Living Single > 41
Laban's Place > 59
Sister, Sister > 63
Under One Roof > 73
Me and the Boyz > 80
Hope and Healing > 86
The Real Fresh Prince > 101
Minor Adjustments > 117
Appendix > 123
Selected Bibliography > 138

INTRODUCTION

"**This message will be taken to the whole world. It will knit my people together, and the hearts of the parents will turn in love to their children, and the hearts of the children will turn in love to their parents**" (Malachi 4:6).

What is this message? **FAMILY MATTERS!** That includes all families. The whole human family. As battered and bruised as it is, the family can heal. Your family can heal. There are two essentials, however. The first is faith in the Creator. Family healing is impossible without cooperating with the Creator's divine and natural principles.

The second essential is your willingness to plan your work and work your plan. In short, the requisite for family hope and healing is faith and works. In that order. Faith comes before works. There are some things you won't believe unless you see. But when it comes to family matters, you must believe before you can see healing take place.

You must have faith to believe that the best for your family is yet to come- no matter how hopeless it may appear right now. When you don't exercise faith, your mind gives us a hundred reasons why you can't heal. **Faith** opens your mind to creative suggestions and solutions.

Then, you must also be willing to **work** through denial, procrastination and fear. The scripture says, "faith without works is dead." Faith is not enough if there is no plan of action (work) to address and resolve the challenges of your family. Now when I say work, I mean work! I'm talking about rolling up your family's sleeves and getting down to some serious business (work). I'm talking about an individual or family commitment to lock-in on your family matters, like a pit bull dog locks in on a trespasser's behind, and don't let go until your family matter are resolved! This book is written to give you encouragement for hope and healing. The main focus of this book is to understand, identify and resolve your family matters. Using a "case study," we will exhume and examine the skeletons of a well-known family. We will see that this family resembles all of our families, to a greater or lesser degree. The hope we have is that no individual or family is irrecoverable! But we must return to the source to move forward. Why? Because Family Matters. Hotep,

Kwame Ronnie Vanderhorst

FAMILY MATTERS
1

"I Am the God of Abraham, the God of Isaac, and the God of Jacob" (Exodus 3:6).

Why does the Creator use this three-fold expression? What is the significance for us? I will answer in two words: **Family Matters!** There is no other entity on earth the Creator deems more needed, required, crucial, necessary, critical, integral, pivotal, indispensable, or quintessential, in the development of the individual, society, and the world, than the Family. Anyone or anything that interferes or inhibits maximum family development, undermines the eternal purpose of the Creator for humanity.

Marriage is the honorable institution the Creator ordained to perpetuate Family, yet, more than half of all marriages in the United States end in divorce. Why? **Because families directly affect marriages, and marriages directly affect families!** Later, we will see how true that statement is.

The book of Genesis in the Hebrew scriptures provides valuable insight into family matters, beginning with the 'first' family, whose origin was in the Nile Valley in Africa.[1] One of the primary contributions of the Hebrew scriptures is the genealogy of Genesis 10, which chronicles the families sired by Noah's sons, Shem, Ham and Japheth after the great Deluge.

Because of the disregard of the Creator's divine and natural laws, humankind 'fell,' becoming subject to spiritual and physical death. What becomes apparent almost immediately is the need of hope and healing for the human family. In love, the recovery of the human family became the Creator's primary initiative.

It is said, when humans want to accomplish something, humans look for a method, but when the Creator wants to accomplish an objective, the Creator looks for an individual. In human history, many women and men have been called 'front and center' to fulfill the righteous purpose of the Creator. Abraham became one of many persons called by the Creator to assist in the recovery of the human family.

It is appropriate to note that "Yahweh" (the Creator) called Abraham, the individual. This point is important because it is a common belief that the "Jews" were chosen by Yahweh above all other people on earth. That is not true. When Yahweh called Abraham, there were no such people as Jews, Christians, Muslims, etc. Yahweh did not call a religion. Yahweh called an individual. Yahweh is not a respecter of people or religions. By that, I mean, Yahweh shows no favoritism, partiality, gender or religious preference. Man does that. It's as simple as this: Yahweh did the calling and Abraham got the call.

There is no doubting Abraham's significance in the history of the human family. Of all people, prophets or distinguished personalities after Yahshua the Messiah, Abraham is without a doubt one of the most renowned figures in Hebrew history.

A Different World

Abraham was reared in Chaldea (Genesis 11:26-31). Chaldea, which was populated by the lineal descendants of Ham, the Cushites, was located in South Babylonia of Western Asia.[2] The Cushites migrated from the Nile Valley in Africa to Western Asia (Genesis 10:15-19). Nimrod, the famous son of Cush, built great nations in that region (Genesis 10:8-10). The Shemites, of which Abraham is a lineal descendant, also migrated from the Nile Valley and settled in Western Asia. Abraham was born in the city of Ur in Chaldea. The mainstream print and news media have misled and misinformed the world by giving the impression that the people of Kemet (Egypt) and Western Asia have always been 'white.' It's insinuated that that area has always been inhabited and governed by Jewish and Arab 'whites.' That is deceptive and untrue. The multiethnic region of Egypt and Western Asia (so-called the Middle East) today is not how it was originally. In Abraham's day, there were no 'white' (European) people in that region. There is no historical, archaeological or anthropological evidence to support or verify a 'white' Africa or a 'white' Western Asia before, during, or long after the time of Abraham. 'Black' Africans not only possessed the continent of Africa, but their dominion extended into Western Asia and beyond. Western Asia was land-locked with Africa, (formally known as "Northeast Africa," before the man-made Suez Canal separated it) and was totally populated and governed by 'Black' African people.[3]

Furthermore, it is a fact that African 'Blacks' have dominant genes and whites have recessive genes, making it is a genetic improbability to claim 'white' origin in Africa or Western Asia. If 'whites' were the first family, where did 'Black' people come from? If Europeans were the first people, when or how did African 'Blacks' come on the scene? If Europe is the cradle of civilization, where's the proof? Why is all the scientific evidence for the beginnings of civilization in the Nile Valley in Africa and not in Europe? I address this issue, not for argument sake, but for accuracy and truth. **Acknowledging the truth precedes healing.**

European and Euro-American historians and theologians provided disinformation through print media and so-called Christian art. African historian Dr. John Henrik Clarke said Europeans not only colonized peoples and lands, they also colonized information (in books). This medium was employed to spread the notion that 'Black' African people were cursed and consigned by the Creator to be "hewers of wood and drawers of water." This lie made it easier to justify the European enslavement, colonization and plunder of Africa's valuable human and natural resources.

The so-called "curse of Ham" myth, concocted by European theologians, denied 'Black' Africans any chance of being acknowledged by Yahweh, much less the chance of being called to assist Yahweh in the recovery of the human family. Combine the misuse of the Bible, the bullet, and Michelangelo the 15th century artist, and "abracadabra!"- the facts and faces of Africa and Western Asia become "white!" That is a different world![4]

Of all the inhumanity of man-against-man, people of 'Black' African ancestry continue to experience the most protracted and inhumane treatment than any other group. This reality alone shows that something is terribly wrong with the human family! Dr. Martin Luther King, Jr. said that if we don't learn to live together as a family, we will die apart like fools! There can be one humanity, only when the blood transfusion of truth has been accepted by the whole human family.

To resolve Family Matters, we must know the truth. Healing can only be achieved when our recovery is based on the truth. Truth is not against anyone, only for everyone. Truth, no matter how painful, is essential to resurrect the human family out of the grave of lies that have embalmed our minds.

Hebrews or Jews?

The modern "Jewish" people of today greatly differ from the ethnic and cultural make-up of Africa and Western Asia, both before and during the time of Abraham. Those controlling the state of Israel who are commonly believed to be "Jews" today are primarily eastern and western European Caucasians. History and Hebrew scripture positively identify them as the lineal descendants of Japheth, Noah's youngest son, who migrated and settled in the region now known as Europe. Ashkenaz, the grandson of Japheth (Genesis 10:2-5), has the most influential descendants in Palestine.

The Ashkenazi "Jews" are not lineal descendants of Abraham, because Abraham was of the lineage of Shem, not Japheth (Genesis 11:10, 26, 27). Ashkenazi and other European "Jewish" people converted the Hebrew faith (misnomered Judaism) but are not the 'covenant' people they claim to be. European Japhethites now occupy the so-called state of Israel through their political Zionist incursion, revived by Theodor Herzl in 1896.[5] What we witness in Palestine today is a very "different world" than it was when Yahweh called Abraham.

The original Hebrew people were not "Jews" but African in origin and ancestry. Even the Hebrew language is an Afri-Asiatic Hamitic language. "The Ugaritic tablets unearthed since 1929, make it abundantly clear that the Hebrew language, including its early poetic structures was taken from the earlier Canaanite population. Indeed the Old Testament language is called not Hebrew but the lip or language of Canaan.'"[6] For the record, Canaan was the son of Ham. Abraham was given the designation 'hebrew' by the Canaanites. His descendants would later be called Israelites and centuries later, misnomered as "Jews."

Yahweh did not bypass African people. The truth is, African 'Black' people were the only people at that time populating Africa and Western Asia. Europe, as we know it, would not come on the scene for a few thousand years later. African people are part and parcel of Yahweh's plan of salvation for the recovery of the whole human Family. In fact, Yahshua (popularly called Christ) was of African-Asiatic ancestry. He was a man of color born in Western Asia in Bethlehem of Judea. Yahshua nor His family is of European origin or ancestry as errant western Christian art and theology depict.

This verifiable, historical truth that I cite in this introduction, does not make African people superior to all others; nor are African people inferior as they are purported to be by Western disinformation. The German scientist, Johann Blumenbach, played a major role in poliferating 'white' superiority and 'black' inferiority with his hierarchic classification of the so-called 'races.' He concocted the terms 'caucasoid, mongoloid and negroid.'

Blumenbach theorized that Caucasians (whites) were the "primal or basic human type from which the Negroid and Mongoloid 'degenerated' under different climatic conditions."[7] **The truth is that there is no such thing as race!** If one accepts (actively or passively) Blumenbach's myth of 'race,' then 'racism' is inevitable. There can be no racism without race. Racism is the illegitimate child of 'race.' The scriptures never mention 'race.'

That compounds the problem of Family Matters, as it has to do with modern humanity. Western theologians reinforce Blumenbach's hierarchy of race by teaching that Noah's sons are the fathers of three 'races.' They say, Ham is the father of blacks, Shem is the father of Asiatics and Japheth is the father of whites. But this supposition poses a problem. What was Mrs. Noah? Multicultural? Did she give birth to three sons who were three different 'races?' Impossible! When one understands that the origin of civilization began in the Nile Valley in Africa, it is not difficult to see that there is not three different 'races,' but ONE HUMAN FAMILY that eventually spread throughout the earth.

In the hotter, sunny climates, the melanocyte cells produced more melanin in humans. In colder climates and less direct sun, like the Caucasus Mountains in Europe, where the Japhethites migrated, the melanocyte-stimulating hormone did not need to produce more melanin. Over time, a lightening (whitening) of the skin took place. When Whites experience a prolonged exposure to the sun, though the melanocyte cells are present, they are not reproducing. It is more of a tanning (or burning) that takes place, making Caucasians darker.

The migration and lineal descendants of Ham, Shem and Japheth have all to do with geographical location, and nothing to do with 'race.' Many descendants of Ham remained on the continent of Africa. Some migrated to Western Asia (Northeast Africa), and other parts of the world. Many descendants of Shem migrated to Western Asia. Most of the descendants of Japheth migrated to the area now known as Europe.

The Hebrew scriptures speak of the lineal descendants of Japheth occupying the "Isles of the Gentiles" (Genesis 10: 5). Get an encyclopedia and trace the names of the descendants of Japheth (Genesis 10:2-5) and it will show they now known as Italians, Russians, Greeks, Spaniards, French, Germans, etc. It's ironic that the 'Japhethites' who have converted to 'Judaism' call all others gentiles, when they are the ones who are identified as gentiles in the Hebrew scriptures by descendants and geographical location.

Furthermore, the Hebrew scriptures also reveal that Japhethites would "dwell in the tents (land) of the Shemites" (Genesis 9:27). In 1947, the United Nations granted statehood to Israel. Couple this with the six-day war of Entebbe in 1967, when the Gaza Strip and Golan Heights were captured from the Palestinians. This confirms that Japheth "dwells in the tents" (occupies the land) of Shem. Obviously, there is the need for justice, hope and healing in land of Abraham.

Without an accurate historical-scriptural account, one would assume that the "Jews" are favored by Yahweh above all others. I hope this brief historical sketch motivates us to reexamine the history we have been conditioned to accept as true. There is a lineal delineation between Hebrews and converted 'Jews' (Japhethites) who migrated to Europe.

In the final analysis, each of us is responsible and accountable for understanding and fulfilling our important role in Yahweh's plan for the recovery of the whole human family. Yahweh excludes no one from the human family. All "families" need hope and healing. Abraham's family personifies this truth. Why? Because Family Matters.

The "Calling Out" Of Abraham

The call of Abraham symbolizes but is not limited to Yahweh's great response, which contains both a remedy and a reaffirmation of the eternal purpose for the human family. The discord among Christianity, Judaism, Islam, (all claiming Abraham as their 'father') further impedes the recovery process of the human family. Each of these religions have numerous sects within themselves that differ in teaching or doctrine; all claiming to be the true religion. Abraham was neither Christian, Jew, nor Muslim.

We should note that it was not a religion that Yahweh called Abraham to, but a covenant relationship, to assist in Yahweh's merciful initiative toward humanity (Genesis 17:1-4). Abraham was called by Yahweh and he followed Yahweh, not a religion.

Yahweh claimed to be the "God" of Abraham, not the God of any particular religion or denomination. That might be painful to some of you but nonetheless true.

Genesis chapters 12 and 13 give the account of the "calling out" of Abraham by Yahweh. Here's how Abraham, an Afri-Asiatic Shemite, became a "Hebrew" (as he was called by the Canaanites of that region (Genesis 14:13). When Abraham reached the land of Canaan, he gave his nephew Lot the first choice of settlement. Lot chose the beautiful area of Sodom. Abraham went on the other side of the river. The Canaanite people in that region called Abraham a "hebrew" because the word 'hebrew' means, "the other side." Abraham eventually fathered a son named Isaac, and Isaac fathered a son named Jacob. Jacob's name would later be changed to Israel. That's how Abraham came to be a "hebrew," and the father of the African Hebrew Israelites. Yahweh addresses the Hebrew Israelites as the "God of Abraham, Isaac and Jacob," alluding to the covenant made with Abraham.

The call of Abraham does not place him or his descendants above all other families, nations or peoples. Yahweh had promised Abraham that "all the families of the earth would be blessed" (Genesis 12:1-3). The opportunity for hope and healing as open to the entire human family.

Skeletons

Although Abraham was "called out," he was still a man, a human, (hyphen intended) and susceptible to the temptations, trials and triumphs families experience today. Though Abraham had many successes and accomplishments, his family struggled with enormous moral and emotional challenges! Abraham's family life was a mess! In fact, any rational person would not designate Abraham's family as a model family! You probably would have told your children they couldn't go over Abraham's house or play with his children. That's how serious his family matters were!

Abraham's family is a microcosm of the human family with all its assets and liabilities. You name it, and you can find it in

Abraham's family. Lying, adultery, jealousy, sibling rivalry, resentment, lust, and the list goes on! Most skeletons in his family closet resemble the skeletons in ours. That's why it is ludicrous for people to proliferate this superior-inferior lunacy! When it comes to family matters, the whole human family is "under one roof," whether you are born in a billionaire family or a family living on the streets. We all have family matters that must be addressed and resolved!

Abraham's family brings the worst and the best out of our families. And yet, Yahweh declared, "I am the God of Abraham, the God of Isaac, and the God of Jacob!" Why? Because Family Matters, therefore all families have hope! This is no easy journey, but we don't have to go it alone.

Statements of Reflection on Chapter 1:
1. Families directly affect marriages and marriages directly affect family.
2. Yahweh shows no favoritism, partiality, gender or religious preference. Man does that.
3. The mainstream print and news media have misled and misinformed the world, giving the impression that the people of Kemet (Egypt) and Western Asia have always been 'white.'
4. Combine the misuse of the Bible, the bullet, and Michelangelo the artist, and "abracadabra!" - the facts and faces of Africa and Western Asia become "white!"
5. Dr. Martin Luther King, Jr. said that if we don't learn to live together like 'family,' we will die apart like fools!
6. Healing can replace the sickness of the body, mind and spirit of those who are willing to be rid of all that inhibits individual and family recovery.

IN THE HOUSE
2

"Time passed, but Sarai, Abraham's wife still had not given him any children. So she decided that Hagar, her Egyptian maid, would make a good mother through whom she could have children. She said to Abraham, 'The Lord has still not given us a child, but maybe we could have one through Hagar and begin our family that way. Why don't you go and sleep with her? If you agree, I'll go and talk to her to see what she has to say about it.' Abraham agreed with Sarai. After Sarai talked to Hagar and she agreed, Sarai brought her to Abraham's tent. He slept with her. Hagar did conceive, and when she was sure she was pregnant, she began to feel superior to Sarai and looked on her with disdain. Sarai was distressed and said to Abraham, 'You're the one responsible for this woman's attitude toward me. I brought her to you, and you slept with her and made her pregnant, but you didn't make me pregnant. So now she looks down on me. May Yahweh judge you for what you've done.' Abraham said to Sarai, 'Hagar is still your maid, so do with her whatever you think is best for both of us.' Then Sarai exerted her authority as Abraham's legitimate wife and told Hagar that she was still her maid, but Hagar refused to serve Sarai and ran off into the desert (Genesis 16:1-6 /CWB)."

"And Yahweh said to Abraham, 'As for your wife Sarai, I have changed her name. You will no longer call her Sarai, but Sarah, which means Princess. I will bless her, and she will give birth to a son and become the mother of nations, including princes and kings.' Abraham, still bowed with his face to the ground quietly laughed and thought to himself, 'How can a man nearly a hundred years old with a ninety-year-old wife have a baby.' Then Abraham said to Yahweh, 'Why not let Ishmael be our offspring and pass

18 In The House

the covenant on to him?' Yahweh answered, 'Sarah , your wife, will have a baby boy, and she will call him Isaac, meaning Laughter. I will pass on my covenant to him and to his descendants. Now as far as Ishmael is concerned, I understand your concern, and I will bless him also. I will make him fruitful and greatly increase his descendants. He will be the father of twelve great rulers, and his descendants will become a great nation. But I will make my covenant with you and with Isaac who will be carried by Sarah and be born about this time next year.' With this, Yahweh finished speaking with Abraham and left him still bowed with his head to the ground (Genesis 17:15-22/CWB)."

It's hard to tell what some families are really all about outside of their homes. Growing up, most parents probably told their children, "don't you go out here and act a fool or else!" Many of us knew how to "act" when we were in public.

When I would visit some of my friends, I noticed that they would never invite me in their house. I would have to wait until they came outside. I still wonder to this very day, what they didn't want me to see or know. The truth is, there is something in all of our homes (families) that we don't want anyone to see or know. No family is immune to family matters. The pompous people who mouth the rhetoric of getting back to traditional "family values" have serious problems in their families. (They pay people plenty of money to hide their skeletons!) Well, it's time to go "in the house" of Abraham.

Abraham's marriage and family was a trip! Abraham married a woman named Sarai. She was constantly depressed from not being able to bear a child for Abraham. It was an embarrassment to be barren and an Eastern woman could become the object of humiliation if she did not bear a son for her husband. So Sarai came up with an idea. She offered Abraham her Egyptian servant Hagar to bear a son for her. (This was before artificial insemination, so Abraham would have to have sexual intercourse with Hagar to make this happen).

Family Matters 19

Abraham, unwisely and without the permission of Yahweh, consented.

Hagar gave birth to Abraham's first son. He was named Ishmael. When you read the scriptural account (Genesis 16), the antagonism between Sarai and Hagar was intense and was brimming with resentment! Sarai's jealous mistreatment of Hagar and Hagar's sarcastic taunting responses were soap operas in themselves!

This whole episode was the result of bad decisions made in the house. Often, in the time of passion, things are said or done where the consequences are not fully considered. Instead of remedying the situation, it is exacerbated. Relationships that were once healthy become strained.

Sarai finally gave birth to a son. He was named Isaac. When there are two women--whose children are fathered by the same man--living in the house, it inevitably leads to some interesting dynamics, to say the least! More sparks flew between Sarai and Hagar; so much so that Sarai appealed to Abraham to kick Hagar and Ishmael "out the house." Abraham eventually complied, but it pained him to his heart because Ishmael was his first son and he loved him.

This home was preoccupied with the tension between Sarai, Hagar and Abraham, that their children became emotionally unstable. In this setting, the children did not escape unscarred! As they encountered discord and hostility in the house, their ability to maintain stable relationships was adversely affected. The boys suffered some emotional problems as youths and adults. Moral weakness was also be a problem later in life. In short, these boys became maladjusted adults. Someone once said, "It is easier to build a boy than it is to mend a man!"

Just think, Sarai encouraged her husband to get another woman pregnant; such decisions put an enormous strain on their marital relationship. This incident cannot be written off as inconsequential. The "oneness" of the marital relationship is so thorough, that sexual intercourse with another partner hurts down in the soul! It's like a dagger thrust into the heart of the marriage and family! The proof is in the consequences that their children reaped, which we will examine shortly.

Had Abraham any idea that having sexual intercourse with a woman other than his own wife would lead to his lamentable family matters, he probably would have chosen to wait on Yahweh to open Sarai's womb. Abraham's human nature won out over faith in Yahweh's covenant with him. Now Isaac and Ishmael would reap what their parents had sown!

We do not have a choice of what family we are born into. The ideal family would be one that is spiritual, balanced, loving, prosperous, has a sense of humor, hard working, intelligent, and community-involved. The reality is that in between these positive attributes are neglect, abuse, addiction, dishonesty, infidelity, poverty, health problems and a host of other family matters children are born into. It's even worse when a child's problems are the result of poor decisions and mistakes by their parents. For example, fetal alcohol syndrome affects children across all ethnic lines. This is unmistakably a parental transmission the child inherits from the parent.

Unfortunately, Ishmael and Isaac had no idea that their own family matters would be plagued with similar difficulties and uncertainties, when they became parents.

Commentary

This narrative exposes many problems in the house of Abraham. There is lack of faith in the Creator, depression, infidelity, poor decision making, Sarai's physical challenges, Abraham's other woman, and a host of other family matters. All these played a detrimental part "in the house" of Abraham and Sarai. But I'm not going to focus on them. I believe (and this is just my thinking) that the least acknowledged, but a more relentless causative that sets the stage for many tragic family matters is **obsession**.

Obsession is a life, marriage and family destroyer. Obsession is like the "cause" of a fire that is finally discovered after picking through the rubble and ruin of a home. Obsession has done as much damage to marriages and families as fire has done to homes! Think about it. Some of the most disturbing marriages and devastating divorces my wife and I have seen have been in relationships primarily involving young couples. We have watched debt (one of the children of obsession) take the joy and passion out of people's marriage. They can't even enjoy the accouterments that keep them in debt because they have to work so much to keep them! The subtle point is that obsession only needs one partner, and "there goes the family!" Obsession is parasitic. It draws the life-blood out of relationships, marriages and families.

Many partners, parents and spouses are obsessed with controlling others. Obsession gives birth to child abuse, spouse abuse, drug usage, anorexia, racism, pornography, suicide attempts, and emotional 'cripples,' just to name a few. Jealousy is one of obsession's oldest children. Debt is also an offspring of obsession. So is, adultery, fanaticism, and all of its other 'sibling rivalries' that exacerbate family matters.

Obsession is not rational; it never was, and never will be. I define obsession as an irrational inward reaction to outward stimuli. That may seem too simple to some of you, but think about it. Societal influence is threatening in many ways, especially to individuals, marriages and families. Society (outside stimuli) sets unreasonable standards for individuals, marriages and families and then judges you by them. Take "success" for example. Just think of all the 'things' society says a person must have or do to be "successful." If you buy into society (outside stimuli) as the standard, you can easily become obsessed with something in life. Unbalanced to say the least.

One of the blessings that I received in life was that I wasn't parented to believe society sets the standards I must follow to accomplish so-called success. My standard didn't come from "outside," but from "in the house." A scripture I memorized as a child, redirected my thought processes, not toward success, but to the Creator: "Trust in the Lord with all thine heart; and lean not unto thine own understanding. In all thy ways acknowledge Him, and He shall direct thy paths" (Proverbs 3:5,6). Instead of the standard society sets, I had an inward standard that set my response to society (outward stimuli). This was the result of my mother's desire to establish a home based on spiritual and balanced character development.

Every morning, before my two sisters, my brother and I left for school, my mother would always say, "Remember whose children you are. Number one, you are a child of God, and number two, you are a Vanderhorst. Don't do anything to bring any reproach on those names." I still picture her today, standing in the doorway, holding the screen door open, saying those words as we walk down the driveway. We knew who we were and we were confident in our abilities.

If parents do not instill spirituality as the standard for their child(ren), then society will set the standard. Without a principled inward response to outside stimuli, a child may become an unstable youth or an obsessed adult.

I looked up the word obsession in the dictionary. It says, "a persistent disturbing preoccupation with an often unreasonable idea or feeling." Obsession also connotes a need for quick solutions. Sarai's obsession was having a male child by Abraham. Abraham's unprincipled response to her need for a quick solution compounded the problem. Abraham and Sarai were probably good people, but good people don't necessarily make good decisions or good parents; especially if one or both of them are obsessed with something in life.

Finally, obsession causes individuals, marriages and families to "build off the line." I watched an elderly African man lay brick when I was a young boy. He had a long chalky string called a plum line. I asked him the purpose of that chalky string that he kept putting between his thumb and forefinger and letting it snap against the brick, imprinting the brick with chalk. He said, "without this, you can build off the line." He meant that without a plum line, the home could be built crooked from its foundation. All it takes is one person, an obsession, a need for a quick solution, and the life, marriage or family can "build off the line." This was the house that Abraham and Sarai built. This is the house Abraham, Sarai and Hagar's children were born into. This became the foundation of their children's home.

Spiritual Reality or Obsession?
As an individual or parent, are you obsessed with anything? Be honest. Years ago, I read a small book written by a Chinese theologian named Watchman Nee. The book was entitled, Spiritual Reality or Obsession. What I distilled as the concept from Nee's book was this: You can be in the presence of someone for five minutes and tell whether they have reached spiritual reality. If they haven't, it's because they are obsessed with something in life.[8] That's deep!

I tested this concept simply by actively listening and observing people I know, and it's true! Either we have reached spiritual reality or we are obsessed with something in life. I've already talked about obsession and its consequences. What then is spiritual reality? It certainly does not mean to be religious. Religion comes by profession. Spiritual reality comes by practice. Many people are religious but not spiritual. Many people profess but don't practice.

I define spiritual reality as the consistent practice of the truth by our words, thoughts, deeds and actions based on spiritual and natural principles (laws). Spiritual reality comes by living according to the Creator's divine and natural laws. The alternative is being obsessed with something in life.

Individual, marital and family matters usually increase when we do not live according to the Creator's divine and natural principles. If you are not open to this reality, your efforts will only be temporary.

How can one be out of harmony with the Creator and the laws of nature and expect to be helped or healed? The Creator has equipped nature with fixed laws to sustain life. If oxygen 'decided' to rebel against the Creator, humankind would not survive five minutes! If the sun 'rebelled' and moved one degree away, we would freeze to death; or one degree closer, we would burn up! Even nature follows its Creator's natural laws. How much more, should humans?

The Creator said, "each seed bears after its own kind" (Genesis 1:11,12). Another scripture says, "we reap what we sow" (Galatians 6:7). That's why parents must study, obey and teach the divine and natural laws (of nature) to their children. They are of utmost importance to the future of our progeny. When parents disregard nature, its laws, and its benefits, children do not truly understand cosmology; that is, the law of cause and effect. Consequently, it is more difficult for them to understand that their decisions today affect their life and relationships tomorrow.

The studying laws of nature with our children also assists families in strengthening their relationships by understanding ontology. Ontology is the study of how things exist (live in relation to other living things). All life is interdependent. No life can exist alone. We need each other. Parents must teach children the importance of using their knowledge, skills, gifts and talents to place the interests of their family and community above their own selfish interests. Children should learn at an early age that life is sacred and should be respected, not violated.

Learning the laws of nature reveal teleology as well. This means there is a design and purpose for all creation. Insight from studying nature's design and composition can show children that they have a special purpose in life. Once children understand their purpose in life, they will be able to identify anyone or anything that contradicts with their purpose and have a better chance to reject their appeal. Whoever tries to live independent of the laws of nature will certainly experience physical death.

Likewise with divine laws. Divine laws are designed so that humans could live in harmony with the Creator and each other. They are summed up in 10 Spiritual Principles (also called the Ten Commandments) in Exodus 20:1-17), but not limited to them. One can imagine how different society would be if we lived by those

10 Principles! Living out of harmony with divine principles have lead to spiritual death, undeniably evident in the inhumanity in the world. Family matters in all its forms, is the greatest proof that we are living outside of the Creator's divine principles. When we obey the Creator's divine principles, abuse stops; crime stops; racism stops; drugs stop; loneliness, bitterness, war and hypocrisy, stops. And hope begins, healing, peace, unity and love all begin.

True hope and healing for individual, marital and family life are byproducts of cooperation. Hope and healing comes by the principles the Creator has established for humanity to live by; not by the "I did it my way" mentality. This is how we reach spiritual reality! This is also how we are rid ourselves of obsession. Furthermore, this puts us on track to becoming balanced and adjusted individuals and families.

There are many who have chosen to live in harmony with the Creator living in harmony with divine and natural principles. After being in their presence for five minutes, you should be able to recognize this. Their spirit is positive and uplifting. You will never leave their presence untouched, discouraged, or unloved. They live their life like an open book. No ulterior motives, no hidden agendas. Deeper still, the "fruit" of their Spirit is love, joy, peace, patience, kindness, goodness, faithfulness, gentleness, and self-control. When these divine principles are lived out in your family life, just think what kind of home you would have!

I hasten to say that this does not give license to judge anyone. All of us are still learning, growing and becoming what we will finally be. And certainly, none of us can judge another's motives. Yet, our words, thoughts, deeds and actions are indicative of the reality we have chosen to prioritize at a given time in life. Reaching spiritual reality is not an end or conclusion to indicate "we have arrived" at a lofty spiritual plateau. It only means that we have prioritized truth through spiritual and natural principles to govern our relationship with the Creator, ourselves, others and our environment. Spiritual Reality or Obsession? That is the question to be answered.

Abraham and Sarai did not prioritize spiritual and natural principles in their decision-making concerning a son. Whenever spiritual and natural principles are disregarded, chaos (obsession) inevitably follows. Now here is my main point in this first narrative. We don't make decisions for ourselves alone. We make decisions for the future of our families, even before our children are born. We make decisions for the future of our families based on our past and present choices and decisions. They can be positive or negative, depending upon the foundation our house is resting on: Spiritual reality or obsession. We must teach this to our children, even using our mistakes and experiences as object lessons, if necessary, to reinforce this truth!

We make decisions for our children even before we become parents! A crack-smoking parent is making a decision for their child, even before she or he becomes a parent. Crack babies testify to that fact! A cigarette-smoking, liquor-drinking parent makes decisions for their children before they become parents. Fetal alcohol syndrome, low birth weight, and a host of other pre/postnatal problems are the result. A gambling parent; a promiscuous parent; a manipulative, scheming parent; all are decisions made for our children before we become parents! All these are obsessions. Abraham and Sarai, (as well as some of our parents), gave their children "a long row to hoe."

Conversely, those of us who are guided by truth through spiritual and natural principles also make decisions for our children before we become parents. Although spiritual and natural principles may not necessarily yield a crop of perfect children, seeds of truth are planted within the child, and if practiced (cultivated), will yield a rich harvest in the form of balanced character. Such character development will also benefit their children even before they get married and become parents.

Abraham and Sarai lived closer to the earth than we do today. They didn't have the modern conveniences we have therefore they depended almost entirely on nature for their physical sustenance. They had a profound knowledge of the laws of nature. They were very familiar with the harvest, planting seeds and crops. We should keep in mind that Yahweh had called Abraham for a special reason and as Abraham depended upon Yahweh's word and guidance, his family would reach its maximal character development and material prosperity. Abraham's family had a good opportunity to "build on the line." But unless this knowledge was practiced they would reap many regrets. Similarly, we will come to regret many things throughout life's course if we fail to practice this knowledge.

Personal growth and positive character development does not spring up overnight. It takes a while to cultivate a good character, but it can all be uprooted with one foolish decision; one unfaithful act. The saddest reality of this narrative is to see a parent's negative lifestyle, choices or vices spring up in their child(ren), and in their children's children. Some may take a lifetime to uproot. This was the reality of Abraham and Sarai. They sowed a seed and reaped a harvest of family matters in their children. Remember, fruit does not fall too far from the tree! It's not my objective to elicit guilt or blame anyone for past or present choices and decisions. I want this to be clear from the beginning.

The vehicle I'm using is my love for my family, my people and the whole human family. My destination is hope and healing for all our families. I'm just readjusting the 'rearview mirror' to help us reflect on what has happened behind us; the side view mirrors to see what is alongside of us; and then the headlights, to shine the light of truth on where we are heading.

Statements of Reflection on Chapter 2:
1. The truth is, there is something in all our homes (families) that we don't want anyone to see or know.
2. No family is immune to family matters.
3. Often, in the time of passion, things are said or done where the consequences are not fully considered. Instead of remedying the situation, it exacerbates it. Relationships that were once healthy become strained.
4. The ideal family would be one that is spiritual, balanced, loving,

prosperous, sense of humor, hard working, intelligent, and community-involved. The reality is that in between those positive attributes are neglect, abuse, addiction, dishonesty, infidelity, poverty, health problems and a host of other family matters children are born into.

5. I believe (and this is just my thinking) that the least acknowledged, but one of the more relentless causative that sets the stage for many tragic family matters is **obsession**.

6. Obsession is parasitic. It draws the life-blood out of relationships, marriages and families.

7. If parents do not instill spirituality to set the standard for their child(ren), then society will set the standard. Without a principled inward response to outside stimuli, a child may become an unstable youth or an obsessed adult.

8. I define spiritual reality as the consistent practice of our words, thoughts, deeds and actions guided by truth through spiritual and natural principles (laws).

9. When parents disregard nature, its laws, and its benefits, children do not truly understand cosmology; that is, the law of cause and effect. Consequently, it is more difficult for them to understand that their decisions today affect their life and relationships tomorrow.

10. The laws of nature also assists our children by strengthening their relationships when they understand ontology; that nature and humanity are interdependent and they benefit more by practicing interdependence by using their knowledge, skills, gifts and talents through placing group interests above individual interests; and that life is sacred.

11. The laws of nature reveal teleology. That means there is a design and purpose for all creation.

12. Once children understand their purpose, they will be able to identify anyone or anything that contradicts with their purpose and have a better chance to reject their appeal.

13. Whoever tries to live independent of the laws of nature will certainly experience physical death.

14. Divine principles are for humans to live in harmony with the Creator and each other.

PARENTHOOD
3

"At this time Isaac had left Lahai Roi. he was living in southern Canaan. One evening he went out to the field to think. As he looked up, he saw camels coming. Rebekah looked and saw Isaac. Then she jumped down from the camel. She asked the servant, 'Who is that man walking in the field to meet us?' The servant answered, 'That is my master.' So Rebekah covered her face with her veil. The servant told Isaac everything that had happened. Then Isaac brought Rebekah into the tent of Sarah, his mother. And she became his wife. Isaac loved her very much. So he was comforted after his mother's death. (Genesis 24:62-67 /New Century Version).

"When Isaac was 40 years old, he married Rebekah. Rebekah was from Northwest Mesopotamia. She was Bethuel's daughter and the sister of Laban the Aramean. Isaac's wife could not have children. So Isaac prayed to Yahweh for her. Yahweh heard Isaac's prayer, and Rebekah became pregnant. While she was pregnant, the babies struggled inside her. She asked, 'Why is this happening to me?' Then she went to get an answer from Yahweh. Yahweh said to her, 'Two nations are in your womb. Two groups of people will be taken from you. One group will be stronger than the other. The older will serve the younger.'

And when the time came, Rebekah gave birth to twins. The first baby was born red. His skin was like a hairy robe. So he was named Esau. When the second baby was born, he was holding on to Esau's heel. So that baby was named Jacob. Isaac was 60 years old when they were born. When the boys grew up, Esua became a skilled hunter. he loved to be out in the fields. But Jacob was a quiet man. he stayed among the tents. Isaac loved Esua. Esau hunted the wild animals that Isaac enjoyed eating. But Rebekah loved

Jacob" (Genesis 25:20-27 /NCV).

I've never seen a sad wedding. Some marriages are sad, but not weddings. You can hear the buzz of excitement as the audience awaits the appearance of the bride. The groom stands waiting in anticipation of a marriage made in heaven. **But wedding ceremonies don't make marriages.** Wedding ceremonies only make a male and female- husband and wife. The parents of the bride and groom make the marriage. You have to think through what I'm saying. Marriage doesn't start at the altar. A healthy or unhealthy interpretation of marriage begins in the home. Parenting (upbringing) sets the stage for marriage. Before a couple reaches the altar, the 'marriage mold' has already been made. If parents rear their children with a healthy and positive understanding of relationships, the opposite sex, trust and responsibility, that increases the likelihood of them having a strong marriage. Especially, if both spouses are reared this way.

I don't want to infer that a sad marriage is the sole result of poor parenting. It is not. Nor do I conclude that a person with a 'bad' upbringing cannot have a good marriage. They can, if they acquire the knowledge and skills that lend to a wholesome marriage. My point is that we should not underestimate how parenting (upbringing) influences a child's concept of marriage even before he or she gets to the altar.

As Abraham and Sarah cuddled their new-born son Isaac, Isaac's future marriage and family problems was far from their minds. Ishmael was thirteen years old when Isaac was born.

It is probable that Abraham and Sarah had not wholly resolved their family matters, especially since Hagar and Ishmael (Abraham's first son) were still living with them. Tension was always in the house. It was Abraham's tragic decision that put him in the middle of volatile confrontations.

Though Sarah made the suggestion of impregnating Hagar, he didn't have to agree to it. He must now share in the responsibility of what transpired in the house. There are some choices and decisions we have made that we can never undo, and when the consequences rear their ugly head, we know why and how they originated. Choices and decisions (good or bad) become personified in a sense. They take on a life of their own. We can do what we want, but we will live on to experience the consequences. Right Abraham?

And of course, Sarah and Hagar had not patched up their differences. The cynicism and resentment was so thick in the house you could cut it with a knife! Their antagonism was the type that would have made the Ricki Lake Show! It would be entitled: I Had A Baby By Her Husband With Her Permission And She Treats Me Like Dirt! Ricki would get some big ratings to have Abraham, Sarah and Hagar on her t.v. tabloid show!

Now that Sarah had her baby boy, things got worse in the house. Each mother was vying for Abraham's affections and trying to have their son favored most by Abraham. This went on for some time. One day, Sarah caught Ishmael making fun of Isaac and she was livid! She stormed to Abraham and demanded that he kick Hagar and Ishmael out the house! Abraham was despondent because he loved Ishmael. But he finally consented and regrettably put them out. Hagar and Ishmael would eventually settle in the desert of Paran. Some years later, Hagar, who was Egyptian, found an African wife for Ishmael in Egypt (Genesis 21:8-20). We don't hear from Ishmael anymore until Abraham dies (Genesis 25:7-9).

How did this soap opera of a home affect Isaac? More than Abraham and Sarah would ever know! Isaac carried a lot of 'baggage' into his marriage with Rebekah. (And later we'll see that Rebekah had her share as well). Isaac is a victim of circumstances he had no control over. Yet, he will suffer the consequences of his parent's choices and decisions. It's not fair, but it's true. All of us reading this book are victims of circumstances that were beyond our control. And guess what? Our children will become the victim or the beneficiary of our choices and decisions! That's what I mean when I say, weddings ceremonies don't make marriages, parents of the bride and groom make the marriage. How we parent our children will have a significant influence on their individual, marital and family life. Parenting can make or break a marriage! How we parent our children can also increase or decrease family matters. If some of you think I'm coming down too heavy on parenting, where else can I begin? The African proverb says, "The hand that rocks the cradle rules the world." That may be true. My proverb is, wedding ceremonies don't make marriages, the parents of the bride and groom makes marriages.

Isaac's marriage started with a fascinating story of how his servant found and selected Rebekah for him (Genesis 24). There are marriages that start out good, **but sooner or later, 'upbringing' surfaces, and all unrecognized or unresolved family matters, find their way into your life, marriage and family!**

It is sobering to see similar character traits and behaviors Isaac received from his father Abraham surface in his own marriage and family. Even Abraham's lie becomes Isaac's lie. Isaac told the same lie as his father in a similar situation.

During Abraham's journey, he rested near the town of Gerar. While there he was asked if Sarah was his wife. Abraham, in fear of his life said, "She is my sister." So Abimelech, king of Gerar, sent for Sarah to make her his wife. Fortunately, the truth was made know to Abimelech, and Sarah was restored to Abraham before Abimelech had sexual intercourse with her. (See Genesis 20:1-18). When Abraham told that lie, Isaac was not even born.

Many years later, Isaac was travelling through the same area and stopped at Gerar. He too was asked was Rebekah his wife. Isaac, fearing for his life, told the same lie his father had told; "She is my sister." Again, the truth was revealed and Rebekah was not taken from Isaac. (See Genesis 26:6-11). "Where did that lie come from? Is Abraham's traits 'surfacing' in Isaac? Is the adage true- "Like father, like son?"

Even before Isaac's wife Rebekah delivered the twins, there were signals of trouble to come. The children "struggled together within her." The Hebrew verb "struggle" is expressive of a violent internal commotion, as if the unborn twins had been constantly tussling with each other in her womb.

The attitudes, temperament and lifestyles of their twins confirmed her difficult prenatal experience. Esau grew up with severe emotional problems. He was moody, predictable and wild, and occasionally had violent outbursts. meanwhile, Jacob was a homebody; quiet, ruthlessly ambitious, cold and calculating, like his mother (Genesis 25:19-34).

In Isaac's home, favoritism and partiality prevailed, just as it did when he was growing up. Sarah favored Isaac over Ishmael. Likewise, Isaac loved Esau, while his wife Rebekah loved Jacob. "Isaac loved Esau..but Rebekah loved Jacob." To top it all off, Rebekah had Jacob deceive and lie to Isaac in his old age so that Jacob would receive the birth- right (inheritance) and blessing (family leadership) from Isaac. The birthright and blessing were reserved for the eldest son of the family; Esau was the first born twin. As a result of being deceived by Jacob, Esau became so angry with his brother that he swore to kill him as soon as the days of mourning his father's death were ended! (Genesis 27). Rebekah feared for Jacob's life and sent him away to her brother Laban in Padanaram. Rebekah never saw Jacob again.

What is undeniably evident is a "visiting of the consequences of the parents upon the children." (Exodus 20:5). I will address this reality at greater length later in this book. The unrecognized and unresolved family matters of Isaac and Rebekah's upbringing have found their way into their children. It's only a matter of time. And, unfortunately, the same happens to us.

Physical features between parent and child are more readily identifiable. Because of my nose, mouth, and hairline, people who know my father say, "I'm Jesse's boy." Children are the recipients of their parent's physical characteristics. The same goes for character traits. All of us can identify negative character traits that we have received from our parents. Traits that you can't whip out! There are positive traits too. We must develop those traits.

What many of us fail to realize (until it's too late) is that negative traits are permitted to perpetuate themselves generation after generation. Many of you see traits of yourself in your children (some in your grandchildren) that you struggled with as a child or youth. Attitudes, temperament and other negative character traits we receive from parents, don't take long to surface in the child(ren). These traits must be dealt with as soon as they are recognized. If they go unrecognized or unresolved, they are usually cultivated (over the years) to our detriment.

This aspect of parenting is virtually overlooked in child rearing. Even if some negative traits are recognized, the methods that most parents use unfortunately includes blaming the child in some way, and punishing him or her for having the characteristics. What went on "in the house" of Isaac, as well as Rebekah's, takes form in the lives of their children.

Commentary

Most parents parent like their parents, unless you choose to parent differently. Parents make parents, though most parents aren't parented to rear their children to be parents. I was going to let you figure that out but I'll explain what I mean. Food, clothing, shelter, music lessons, financing education, etc., are on the front end of parenting. That's basic. But what is usually left out of parenting children is rearing children who may one day be parents. Most parents don't parent to make parents. This is not to say our children have to be parents. That's their choice. But should they become parents, shouldn't they know how to parent? Parenting does not come by osmosis. Parents make parents.

Are you preparing your children to parent your grandchildren? That may be one of the reasons we have such an epidemic of parenting grandparents today? Grandparents who can't be called grandma and grandpa because their children are in drug rehab, in prison, in the grave, or still in the streets flirting, and they have to parent their grandchildren for the next 15-20 years!

One of the goals my wife and I have is to rear our daughters to be parents. (Hopefully, after they are married). How do we plan to pull that off? By the way we parent them. Children become "parents" long before they become parents of their own children, and it has nothing to do with pregnancy. It has to do with how parents rear them.

Parenting is not innate. If it was, we would be doing a better job of it as a collective. Parenting is caught and taught, in that order. Though a female has the ability to be a mother, she does not automatically possesses what it takes to be a parent. These are two different realities. A male may become a daddy, but may never become a parent in the true meaning of the word. The words, daddy, mommy and parent are not synonymous. One is biological, the other is psychological. Sperm and egg are biological; parenting is psychological. Only parents 'make' parents.

Abraham became a father. Sarah became a mother. But who parented the children? I'm trying to take us to the next level in our thinking because the true understanding of parenthood is taken for granted, taken out of context. Attaching labels to people don't make them that. Having children don't make parents; only mothers and fathers. Being present in the home does not make one a parent.

Parenting is not biological. Copulation is biological, but it doesn't produce parents; only a child. If parenting (in the true meaning of the word) was simply biological, why are so many people unattached to their parents? As I stated in my book, Rearing African Children Under American Occupation, "Parenting is the interaction of your thought processes. How you think is how you parent."

Spiritual parenting is a distinct mental function of the thought processes that expresses itself in word, thought, deed and action through obedience to the Creator's divine and natural principles in relationship with one's children.

I'll say it again: Parenting is caught and taught; in that order. Parents can talk all they want but children usually imitate what they see. Our parents (or whoever reared you) are our 'point of reference.' We can only refer back to how they handled situations in the home.

How did your parents handle the washing of dishes in your home? Growing up, my two sisters, my brother, and myself rotated on a weekly basis washing dishes. Many of you grew up under that same rotation. Now my children rotate washing dishes. More than likely, their children will rotate washing dishes.

How did your parents talk to you when they got upset with you? Did they holler, belittle or speak softly? How do you talk to your children when you're upset with them? More often than not, the same way your parents talked to you, unless you have made it a point to talk to your children differently. My point is that we learn to parent by observing our parent's methods, reactions and responses. We learn to parent from our parents.

I tell my daughters some of the very same things my mother told me: "Do a job right the first time and you won't have to do it over again." "Learn to do things without being told. See what needs to be done and do it." All that and more, I 'caught' and was 'taught' from my mother. I use many of her positive methods in parenting. She is a very detailed person as it pertains to work. So am I. That was 'caught and taught' from her. She called it, "having an eye." A lot of people don't have "an eye." They miss the little things that make the difference between good and great work. I want my daughters to have "an eye." They can acquire this trait as I teach them the importance of work, or by observing how I work.

What am I alluding to? My mother parented me to parent, not simply to be a daddy. I observed her reactions and responses to so many situations in life. She is class all the way. One Sabbath after church, a lady said something derogatory to my mother in the church lobby and my brother and I wanted to confront that lady! We were young, not even teens at the time, and we thought that nobody should talk to our mother like that and get away with it. My mother sent me and my brother to the car. We sat there angry and crying. We wanted that lady! As we were riding home, we asked our mother why she didn't respond or defend herself. My mother, whose insight and compassion is phenomenal only said, "Consider the source." We couldn't understand it then. But not long after, the lady was put in a mental hospital. She wasn't well mentally and my mother knew it.

It is her responses to many challenges in life that I 'caught' from her. But she also 'taught.' With her, there was always a teachable moment. She never responded, "Because I said so." She always took time to explain 'what,' and she taught by showing us 'how' it should or could be done. I don't remember any work we did in the house or out in the yard that she didn't show us how to do it first.

Parenting is caught and taught. It is lifestyle first and lessons second. When a parent's lifestyle is honorable and principled, then their lessons (words) have more meaning, more lasting impact. This is parenting to parent at its best. But it goes both ways. Things are caught and taught that negatively affect a child's future parenting. The more I look and listen to parents, and the way some of them parent their children, I shudder because they don't have the faintest idea that they are parenting to parent. They don't wake up each day and realize that they are their child's point of reference, as it relates to parenting. They haven't understood parenting is psychological and must be engaged at the level of the thought processes. Parental lifestyle (methods and behavior) is simply the byproduct of how a parent thinks.

I was watching a popular t.v. talk show and the host said to one of his guests, "I am tired of hearing people refer to their upbringing as an excuse to abuse their children! When are you going to stop it and take responsibility for what you have done and quit blaming someone because you were abused when you were young!" The host got a rousing applause from the audience. My response is, what he said might sound good, but it did not erase that guest's past. Victims are not responsible for their abusive upbringing. Their abusers are the one who are to be held responsible. The victims are just the recipients of it. What the victims, the talk show host, the audience, and the abusers must know is that all unrecognized or unresolved family matters will, in some way or another, find their way into the lives, marriages or their families! What they need help with is becoming accountable for seeking help so that they can heal. I get tired of insensitive and self-righteous people blaming victims.

The past is always present, and most parents parent like their parents unless they learn to parent differently or resolve their past challenges through positive intervention. One things for sure, they aren't going to find hope or help on that talk show! The talk show host was bashing people who had no real control over their past. And let's be absolutely clear: resolving family matters is not about blaming but rather about healing. But this cannot be done without considering the source.

Conversely, there are things that my wife and I have chosen to do differently with our children than our parents did with us. We have agreed to approach some situations and responses different than our parents handled them. For instance, we don't hit our children for any reason. I discuss that at length in my book, Rearing African Children Under American Occupation.

Many of our parents did the best they knew how, but parenthood is not static, therefore our methods and responses need periodic review and revision. The truth is, we can't entirely parent our children like we were parented. Although our parents are our point of reference, we have our own individuality, and so do our children. Rearing our children to appreciate their own individuality and adhere to the Creator's natural and divine principles will have a lot to do with their success when living on their own.

Woe to the parents who are more interested in their children make a living than teaching them how to live; especially, "living single." This is the tragic dilemma Jacob was thrust into. Many of our children are forced into living single too early.

Statements of Reflection on Chapter 3:
1. Wedding ceremonies don't make marriages. Wedding ceremonies only make a husband and wife. The parents of the bride and groom make the marriage.
2. If parents rear their children with a healthy and positive understanding of relationships, the opposite sex, trust and responsibility,

that increases the likelihood of them having a strong marriage.
3. There are marriages that start out good, but sooner or later, 'upbringing' surfaces, and all unrecognized or unresolved family matters, find their way into your life, marriage and family!
4. What is undeniably evident is a "visiting of the consequences of the parents upon the children."
5. What many of us fail to realize (until it's too late) is that negative traits are permitted to perpetuate themselves generation after generation.
6. Most parents parent like their parents unless you choose to parent differently.
7. These traits must be dealt with as soon as they are recognized. If they go unrecognized or unresolved, they are usually cultivated (over the years) to our detriment.
8. Children become "parents" long before they become parents of their own children, and it has nothing to do with pregnancy. It has to do with how parents rear them.
9. Daddy, mommy and parent are not synonymous. One is biological, the other is psychological. Sperm and egg are biological; parenting is psychological.
10. Spiritual parenting is a distinct mental function of the thought processes that expresses itself in word, thought, deed and action through obedience to the Creator's divine and natural principles in relationship with one's children.
11. Parenting is caught and taught. It is lifestyle first and lessons, second. When a parent's lifestyle is honorable, then their lessons (words) have more meaning; more lasting impact. This is parenting to parent. But it goes both ways. Things are caught and taught that negatively affect a child's future.
12. Many of our parents did the best they knew, but parenthood is not static, therefore our methods and responses need periodic review and revision.

LIVING SINGLE
4

"As soon as Isaac had finished blessing Jacob, Jacob had barely left when Esau his brother came back from hunting. Esau cooked Isaac's favorite meal and took it into him. 'Eat father and then give me the blessing' (reserved for the eldest son). Isaac said, 'Who are you?' 'I am your firstborn son Esau.' Then Isaac trembled and asked, 'Who brought me the meal that I ate before you came in; and who received my blessing? The blessing is upon him.' When Esau heard his father's words, he cried bitterly and said, 'Bless me please, my father.' Isaac said, 'Your brother Jacob came in and deceived me and took your blessing.' Esau said, 'He is right to be named Jacob, for he has tricked me two times! He took away my birthright and now he has taken my blessing! Father, don't you have a blessing for me?' Isaac answered, 'I have put Jacob in charge of all I possess; there is nothing I can do for you.' Esau replied, 'Father, don't you have just one blessing for me?' And Esau cried (Genesis 27:30-38)."

"And Esau hated Jacob because Jacob took his blessing. Esau vowed, after the days of mourning our father's death are ended, I am going to kill Jacob! Someone told Rebekah of Esau's plan and she sent for Jacob and said, 'Esau is planning to kill you. Do as I tell you and escape to my brother Laban's home in Haran. Stay there until Esau's anger is gone and he has forgotten what you have done to him; then I will send for you. How can I lose (your father) and you at the same time?'" (Genesis 27: 41-45).

In childhood, unconditional love, patience, planning, structure and decision-sharing is vital in the home. Parents and children should have good dialogue and occasional family meetings in the home. This gives the children the opportunity to express themselves and their point of view, hear ideas of other family members, as well as share in the family's collective decision-sharing process. Even when there are disagreements, family members can learn to respectfully agree to disagree.

It doesn't seem as if Isaac and Rebekah communicated well with one another. In fact, their silence on a major family matter became the issue that ultimately tore their family apart. Isaac and Rebekah knew that Yahweh had said, "The elder will serve the younger" (Genesis 25:23). This was a reversal of tradition. The eldest son was to receive the birthright and blessing. The birthright is a "privilege or possession which a person is entitled to by birth." Two-thirds of the land and possessions would go to the eldest son. The remaining one-third would be divided by the rest of the sons. The eldest son also received the blessing. This blessing meant he would become the spiritual leader of the family when the father died. Though Esau was the eldest by birth, Yahweh chose Jacob to carry out the spiritual leadership of the family.

As the story reveals, Jacob got Esua to sell his birthright for some lentil soup. Now he would receive two-thirds of his father's possessions. As for the spiritual leadership, Rebekah devised a plan for Jacob to deceive his blind daddy and steal the blessing.

When Isaac found out what had happened, he was grieved to his heart. First, for disregarding the instructions of Yahweh by deciding to bless Esau instead. Secondly, because his wife and son had lied and tricked him into blessing Jacob.

Had Isaac and Rebekah shared Yahweh's will with their sons, they could have avoided the hurt and hatred that resulted from this family matter. When Esau found out what happened, he went ballistic! He vowed to kill Jacob. Jacob feared for his life. Rebekah packs Jacob's clothes and forces him out the door. He would hide at his uncle Laban's home in Mesopotamia. Rebekah never saw Jacob again.

Commentary

Jacob is living single. He's on his own for the first time in his life. The mamma's boy-turned-fugitive is thrust out into an unplanned single life. Ready or not, here he comes! It's bad enough when a young adult refuses to abide by reasonable home rules and leaves on his or her own. But when it is the parent's wrong-doing that the child has to leave prematurely, who can fathom the far-reaching consequences?

So many children are being thrust out into living single before their time. Some of you left home early, for whatever reason. You had to grow up fast, and often, you learned by trial and much error! I've talked with young people who were put out of the house at 13 and 14 years old. Can you imagine their psychological trauma, especially when they don't have supportive relatives who will take them in? One young man's mother chose between him or her live-in boyfriend. His mother chose her boyfriend and put him on the streets! Likewise, Rebekah put Jacob on the streets before his time.

Young people should feel confident and optimistic when leaving home. They ought to be secure in their cultural identity, individuality, abilities, preparation (which includes formal or vocational education) and plans. Living single, with all of the above, can still cause a young person some anxiety in the beginning. But living single without preparation, self-discipline and good planning is scary and unwise!

Living single is also a prelude to marital and family life. Without a doubt, many habits, good and bad, will carry over. If a person is not focused as a single, it will take great effort to get on track after one gets married. In some areas or instances, one may never fully recover the lost opportunities that were once in abundance. Many spouses who squandered their lives living single, seem to play 'catch-up' all the time as husbands and wives. Blown educational opportunities mean a chunk of time (or finances) have to be diverted during the marriage in order to go back and get a degree or equivalent certification. This time or money could have been invested in another area had that spouse been focused educationally or vocationally while living single.

If the spouse does not make the sacrifice to obtain credentials, underemployment usually results and the spouse is payed far below his or her genius. Thus, it becomes a perpetual financial struggle that drains the marriage. This is just one of a myriad of examples of what happens when young people are forced to leave home before their time.

Living single is a great time to enhance and fine tune character, or a bad time to acquire a reputation. I tell young people, "Character is what you stand for; but reputation is what you fall for. If you don't stand for something, you will fall for anything!" One thing is for certain for those living single- you reap what you sow. Habits formed while living single will come back to help or haunt them not only financially, but also morally, socially and personally, if they start a family of their own.

As I am writing this book, my eldest daughter is beginning the ninth grade. She graduated from the eighth grade as class president and valedictorian. It seems as if it was just yesterday, as a baby, she took naps, laying on my chest. She was so tiny and cute! My youngest daughter is beginning seventh grade. She has a phenomenal mind and loves animals. She plans to be a veterinarian. I didn't realize how fast children grow until I got married and we had our own.

We have our children a very short time. We only have a very short time to prepare them for living single. Wholesome living single is a state of mind first before it becomes a physical reality. The number one essential of wholesome single living is a spiritual base to discern between good and evil, truth and error, faith and feelings, true love and infatuation, and good friends and bad associates. The African proverb says, "When you know who his friend is, you know who he is." Rearing children to be independent thinkers is a primary component of living single. Teaching them good decision-making skills based on principle is equally important.

These are some essentials my wife Janice and I are teaching our daughters in preparation for living single: How to wash clothes and iron, how to do a job well the first time, how to sit and eat appropriately at the table, how everything they do (from house work to homework) is like signing their family name to it and represents the kind of work that rightly represents our family; how to acknowledge when they have been wrong and use a full sentence when making it right, instead of just saying, "I'm sorry;" how to say "Yes Sir, No Sir, Yes Ma'am, No Ma'am;" how not to think they are too old to play with and spend time with younger children when they become teenagers. And, there's more:

How to be a real friend, how to appreciate and acknowledge their family first and foremost; how to share, how to always be truthful; how to think for themselves; how to question authority in the appropriate way and time, how to treat others as they want to be treated, how not to be silent when they need to speak up, how to give a firm handshake and look the person in the eyes; how their special calling on life is to give help and hope to those in need; how to care for and respect their own bodies; how to respect the environment; how to know the difference between needs and wants, how to read and to love reading wholesome books; how to love themselves and their African culture; how to respect all humanity regardless of their ethnicity or belief system; how to accept responsibility for their own choices and decisions; how to eat naturally and use natural herbs and remedies; how to respect the elders and listen to wisdom; how to discipline themselves; how to think optimistically; and how to have faith in the Creator. And we have so much more to teach our daughters before they leave home!

Jacob's experience was just the opposite and his challenges were just beginning at Laban's place. Though he would pull through, it would be through many years of struggling with his inherited and cultivated traits.

Childhood only comes once. As adults, we can't rewind our childhood, dub over it, and record a new one. It becomes a permanent recording in our psyche. By the time a child is five years old, the 'recording' is basically complete. There is a lot of attention given to prenatal physical health and well-being, but too little attention is given to prenatal character development. Not only must mothers-to-be have a good physical health plan, they must also have a plan to begin recording permanent principles in the mind of their child.

Love motivates parents to invest the time and attention necessary to prepare our children for living single. Love requires changing whatever needs to be changed in our homes in order to salvage the short time you have left with your children. Love advises us to turn off the t.v. so that we can create the proper environment for our children to become proficient readers and writers. Love doesn't mind sacrificing for our children to be musically proficient. Learning and practicing with an instrument helps the child to become more disciplined. Love wisely involves others to assist you in the balanced development of your child. Love empowers our children to be community minded, assisting in areas of refinement and self-determination for their people first, and then society.

Jacob left too soon. Since his parents didn't prepare him to live on his own, he had to take on "survival behavior." That is the inevitable behavior for children who leave home unprepared. Jacob had to hustle to live. He had to scheme, con, lie, cheat, steal, to trust no one, and to keep looking over his shoulder for his brother Esau. All the while waiting for his past to catch up with him.

Mother-Son Relationships

Jacob is a victim of his upbringing. His father favored his brother Esau. His mother squandered her opportunity to bring stability and balance to her son's life. Esau stayed home for a while but I can imagine his respect for his mother Rebekah was gone completely. They probably argued to no end. Who knows, he may have never forgiven her for what she did. Now Jacob had to leave before his time. He must bear part of the responsibility for going along with his mother's devious scheme. He's filled with fear and anxiety as he runs for his life!

Mothers need to be prayerful and careful how they rear their sons. The mother-son bond is more than biological. It is psychological too. Most sons will fight at the drop of a hat over their mothers! I don't know any sons who will fight for their fathers if a bully says, "Your father!" But if he says, "Your Mama," it's time to take off the coat! This bio-psychological bond can help or hurt a son in childhood and seriously impede his transition from boyhood to manhood.

It is true that fathers have a role in helping sons become men, but mothers make 'gentlemen.' Because so many mothers are parenting alone in the home, and so much attention is focused on "deadbeat dads" and absent fathers, the predominant role mothers have in the mental-emotional development of their sons is hardly discussed. Mothers have a greater part in developing the manhood of their son at an earlier age than the father does.

A mother takes the lead with her son, especially during those nurturing years. She establishes the mental-emotional stability of the male-child more than the father. Because of her bio-psychological bond, her son is not as cognizant of the father's role as he is of his mother's. He perceives his mother as his primary caregiver. Up until the age of 12, a young boy will primarily identify with his mother. The son eventually discerns his father's role (in the home) as being supportive of his mother's primary initiatives.

The father's role (paying bills, keeping the lights and heat on, etc.,) is not recognized by the son at this young age. That knowledge comes later. The pivotal issue that will make or break the father-son relationship is the son's observation of how his father treats his mother. The father's love and respect or mistreatment and disrespect of his son's mother is indelibly stamped on his son's mind for life. This, believe it or not, is the foundation of the son's relationship with his father. It comes through observation first, then interaction.

Stay here a minute. A father who is present in the home, engaging in sports and other physical activity with his son, is not the tie that binds the father-son relationship. If he doesn't treat his son's mother right, no amount of positive physical interaction, gifts or otherwise, will solidify their relationship. It will be tense and strained.

One of the greatest gifts a father can give to his son is to love his son's mother, or if they are not together, at least, be his mother's friend. If not, it may take a lifetime for that son-father relationship to heal, although, there can never be any reconciliation without confession. This is because the bio-psychological bond between mother and son is stronger at this early stage in his life than it is with his father. Mama has center stage. Dad is in the 'wings' in a supporting role until it's time for him to take center stage.

Let me just add this for mothers who are parenting alone. If your son's father is not positively active in your son's life, your son will observe the men you date. Your son will read them like a book, even at a young age. His discernment is sharp, as it relates to mama. If your 'significant other' mistreats or disrespect you, your son will take note and will grow to despise him and you (for letting it happen). The mental-emotional stability of your children must come first. This will certainly weed out some admirers and 'upgrade' your selection process. You do not want your son to loose respect for you and women in general who permit themselves to be disrespected or mistreated by a man. The man doesn't have to be perfect, but he must be principled. One thing for sure: Your son will read his spirit. He will know whether your date is on the up-and up.

During my mother's nurturing-identification years with me and my brother, our concept of women was developed. A mother is a son's first impression of womanhood. When a mother is principled, spiritual, positive, patient and consistent, (like my mother was) a son can't help but develop a healthy concept of womanhood. Mothers, don't underestimate your power to help or hurt your son in this respect. Your son will usually choose in his life, the kind of woman you are. Not always, but usually. You are his 'female' point of reference.

Live to be the kind of woman you would want your son to marry. I directly attribute my excellent selection of my wife Janice to the healthy concept of womanhood my mother 'lived' and exemplified before me. You only have a few short years to establish his mental-emotional stability and his concept of womanhood; and then your role becomes supportive throughout his life.

When a son's hormones 'kick in,' his identification with his father (a man) becomes predominant. It is essential that he receive consistent, positive male interaction and influence. Many sons may not express it verbally, but they want their biological father at this time, or the father figure they have known. This son-father bonding (depending on the father's relationship with his son's mother) is from age 12 to 18, give or take a year or two. Even if his father has been there all along, this hormonal transition is like a new beginning in their relationship; or should I say, the next level. For the son, this is a bio-psychological transition away from the mother-nurturer to the necessary psycho-relational bonding with father (manhood).

The son wants his father to be there, to come to his games or activities; to be visible to him and his male friends. He wants his father to affirm him in his accomplishments and counsel him in his challenges. This is the time in the son's life where I say, he starts "smelling himself." He needs male hormones (a father or positive male influence) around him. This is a very critical time for a young man. He can (and many do) gravitate to negative male influences. Not that he wants to be negative, but the male identification (hormone) is so strong at this time in his life.

His mother is there, supportive of the father's primary initiative toward his son. Her son still needs and wants her to put on his 'bandages,' but only behind closed doors. No one replaces a mother's hands when a child is wounded (hurt). But he wants his father to help him up outside the house and give him that 'push,' of reassurance when he falls off the bike of life. Daddy has center stage now.

It is also a time when the son's interest in the opposite sex is heightened. This also encourages male identification. It is at this juncture in the son's life that a father who has been respectful to his son's mother really pays dividends. The son has 'caught' his father's lifestyle and behavior, and now he can be 'taught' from a good man's perspective how to love, respect and treat a woman. When a father's lifestyle or behavior has not been on the up-and-up with his son's mother, the son has 'caught' this. If his mother has not surrounded this son's life with positive male influence (his uncles, respectable church or community men, etc.) to be 'taught' otherwise, this son will not be adjusted in his concept of himself or his manhood. He may try to prove his manhood is between his legs instead of in his brain. Sooner or later, he may be the man who mistreats or disrespect some other son's mother and that son will learn to despise him and his own mother. He may become the very person he despised when he was growing up! It's a cycle where low personal worth, abuse, and the like, go round and round.

During this period of male identification, a mother cannot be a father. I often hear mothers who are parenting alone say, "I have to be the mother and the father." You can't be the father and you should stop saying that. It's a man's duty now. You've laid your foundation (positive or negative). All that a mother has modeled concerning womanhood is in cement in the son's psyche. Now you are to do all you can do to have positive male influences in his life. At his time, the son sees his mother as visible and supportive of the father's initiatives. This is a critical time in his life, because the father helps bring to maturation the son's moral and psychological adjustment for manhood. If not, he will have a distorted concept of true manhood. He will learn the street version and his relationships will suffer for it. As the saying goes, "It is easier to build a boy than it is to mend a man!"

As I mentioned earlier, until the age of 12 (plus or minus a year) the mother leads in her son's mental-emotional stability. When the mother-son relationship is loving, mutually respectable and principled, the son not only grows up with a proper concept of himself and his manhood, he also develops the proper concept of womanhood. It is a mother who teaches a son how to love, appreciate and respect women. Being taught to love, honor and respect his mother is the foundation for her son loving, honoring and respecting females in general.

After the father has established the manhood of his son during those teen years, when the son begins to date seriously, and especially toward engagement, the mother comes back front and center in his life. He now wants his mother's female wisdom, insight and perspective to guide him in the appropriate selection of a wife-to-be. He needs his mother to 'look over' the females he brings home.

Not to criticize but to critique from a woman's point of view. In fact, many sons won't just bring home any young lady. When their mother has set a spiritual and principled standard of womanhood, they wait until they have chosen someone with similar qualities before they 'let her in the house!' My point is that it is important for a son to get primary and final confirmation from his mother concerning females he is serious about. Mama's perspective and intuition (her sixth sense) is valued even above his father's. After their son's marriage, depending on the son's circumstances, mama and daddy will take turns in primary or supportive roles toward their son and his family, the rest of their lives.

What I have just addressed is primarily the 'ideal' setting for a mother-son relationship to reach its full maturation. Certainly, the father's role is important to his son, though we will later see his prominence is in the father-daughter relationship. The mother-son relationship will most definitely have an immediate effect on the son living single.

Sad to say, some mothers (like Rebekah), have squandered their once-in-a lifetime opportunity to prepare their sons with the mental-emotional stability and the positive character traits to enhance their living single. Some mothers have manipulated their sons into catering to their own whims and wishes. I know men who will drop everything they're doing to do what mama wants when she calls, but will not lift a finger to respond to his own wife's request! Some mothers willfully play their sons against his own wife and family. Jacob was primed to be an emotionally dependent, irresponsible man. Jacob's mother was deceitful and selfish and did not truly earn any respect or honor from Jacob; only his obedience. It negatively impacted his concept of motherhood and womanhood.

I do not discuss the negative impact of the mother-son relationship to make any mother feel guilty. I do it because it is a reality that cannot and must not be denied. I also include it so those mothers who will acknowledge their mistakes can reconcile any differences with their sons and heal. Rebekah never had that chance to reconcile with her son Jacob. She died a few years later, thus, it was never resolved between the two.

Rebekah was on the 'take' like some mothers. This is the type of mother who doesn't think twice about violating principle. Some mothers know their sons are bringing home 'blood' money and giving it to them but don't say anything, nor do they refuse it. It doesn't matter how he got it or who he hurt to get it! Their selfishness encourages this negative behavior in their sons. But when the son reaps the consequences of his negative lifestyle, the mother has to live with the knowledge that she was part of his problem. Can you imagine how Rebekah must have felt in her quiet reflections concerning how she initiated wrong doing against her husband and son? Can you imagine how Jacob felt about his mother, having to leave home under these unfortunate circumstances?

There are so many other scenarios that damage mother-son relationships. When mothers abrogate principle, most sons grow up with a "love-hate" relationship with mama; they love her but hate what she has done to him, or not done for him. So many children are bitter to this very day because their parents made choices for them and enforced their will upon them to accomplish their self-serving agenda.

The obsession with position and prestige has driven some parents to neglect the needs of their children. They way some children get their parents attention is to get in trouble. Other parents have violated their child and caused a scism they have yet to repent of or resolve. As a result, many grown children could care less if they ever go back home to visit their parents; others are so embittered they don't want their own children to have anything to do with their grandparents. Still for others, the wounds are still deep and open even though they are grown and gone.

Leave and Cleave

Children should not leave the side of their parents and cleave to living single until they have developed internal and external requisites. Character, discipline and responsibility are internal qualities. Skills, expertise (profession or vocation) and economic independence are acquired external necessities. These essentials should be developed by their parent's side.

Please understand what I mean when I say 'by their parent's side.' It is more of a relational proximity, than it is physical. When parent's and children "drift" apart in relationship, as Jacob and his parents had, emotional separation is inevitable.

Even if a child is not living in their parent's home, but the relationship between the parent and child is loving and wholesome, then that child, in essence, remains by the side of that parent, and vise versa. That child may be in a university, three thousand miles away, but parent and child are still in close emotional proximity to each other. In this relationship, the child continues to mature and develop knowledge and skills in preparation for living single.

If that loving and wholesome relationship is lacking, the child may not only leave but will probably cleave to living single before his or her time. When they leave and cleave to living single too soon, they are exposed to all kinds of voices and choices. Because of their emotional immaturity and lack of preparation for living single, they fall victim to devouring enemies.

The child may end up 'shacking' with someone; hanging out with questionable company, wasting valuable years job-hopping, dependent, or drifting with no definite goal in sight. It all depends on the voices they follow or the choices they make.

That's why it's so important to, "Train up a child in the way he or she should go, and when they are older, they will not depart from it." That does not mean a child will not leave; but the peace for parents come when they know they have put within their child a spiritual compass to find their way back 'home.'

The benefits of keeping a child by a parent's side until they are ready to properly leave and cleave are innumerable. There is confidence, stability and an optimism that accompanies that son or daughter who is ready. Parents can rest at night, virtually assured that their son or daughter is 'alright.' Parents also have confidence in their choice of associations and lifestyle.

On the other hand, the child(ren) who leave too soon, for whatever reason, bring anxiety and restlessness to concerned parents. The parents usually don't know where they are, who they hang out with, or what they are doing most of the time.

Though no parent can predict the final outcome, children benefit by their staying by their parent's side until their character and career (purpose in life) are intact.

Cultivated Traits

When children are left alone, or as in Jacob's case, pushed on their own, they cultivate traits that are usually detrimental to living single. These cultivated traits might be the result of unrecognized or unresolved inherited traits, or habits cultivated by personal choice or association. I counseled a young lady who was engaged to be married but her fiance had a drinking problem. She wanted to know what she should do. I told her that was her decision, not mine. I did inform her that if he was a drunk before she married him, nine times out of ten, he would be a drunk after they got married. If he hit her before they got married, nine times out of ten, he would knock her teeth out after they got married! The habits of living single persist in adulthood, marriage and the family unless these cultivated traits are addressed and resolved.

For the record, let me say this: Many of us had a 'good' upbringing, but went out on our own and made some foolish choices. Our parents cannot be faulted. Some of the cultivated traits resulted from not following the principles we were taught as children. Some of us know where or how we veered from Maat (the path of righteousness). We know that because of our upbringing. We have a compass, a point of reference.

With Jacob, as well as with any young adult, a major determinant in living single is knowing their purpose in life. I didn't say it was a final determinant, just a major determinant. Living single is more than working and paying rent. It is also about establishing relationships, choosing associations, responding or reacting to unforeseen situations, locking in to a certain lifestyle.

When parents empower their children with a balanced appreciation of themselves and their **purpose**, their reason for being, it counters identity-confusion and minimizes cultivating negative habits. They will be able to discern when something or someone contradicts their purpose and when to establish relationships that are conducive to their health and well-being.

Associations can make or break a person living single. When parents prioritize character development in the home, they see the importance of monitoring their child's friends. They utilize this opportunity to observe, not judge, their child's associations, affirming them or reasoning with them why they should remain kind but not in the company of that person or group. As a young adult, I cultivated some negative habits simply by associating with the wrong people when living single.

The enemy of all humanity will stop at nothing to keep every child from reaching the purpose they were created to be. But when a child's own parents are his or her primary 'enemy,' it makes it all the worse! Jacob's parents became his 'enemy.' Not only did they not prepared him for living single, but they forced him out of the house to soon! Now, Jacob's is about to leave and cleave to a nightmare.

Statements of Reflection on Chapter 4:
1. Parents and children should have good dialogue and occasional family meetings in the home. This gives the children the opportu-

nity to express themselves and their point of view, hear ideas of other family members, as well as share in the family's collective decision-sharing process.
2. Young people should feel confident and optimistic when leaving home. They ought to be secure in their cultural identity, individuality, abilities, preparation (which includes formal or vocational education) and plans.
3. Living single is also a prelude into marital and family life. Without a doubt, many habits, good and bad, will carry over.
4. Blown educational opportunities mean a chunk of time (or finances) have to be diverted during the marriage in order to go back and get a degree or equivalent certification.
5. If the spouse does not make the sacrifice to obtain credentials, underemployment usually results and the spouse is payed far below his or her genius. Thus, it becomes a perpetual financial struggle that drains on the marriage.
6. Living single is a great time to develop and fine-tune character, or a bad time to acquire a reputation.
7. Habits formed while living single will come back to help or haunt them not only financially, but also morally, socially and personally, if they start a family of their own.
8. Wholesome living single is a state of mind first before it becomes a physical reality. The number one essential of wholesome single living is a spiritual base to discern between good and evil, truth and error, faith and feelings, true love and infatuation, and good friends and bad associates.
9. Rearing children to be independent thinkers is a primary component of living single. Teaching them good decision-making skills based on principle is equally important.
10. Love motivates parents to invest the time and attention necessary to prepare our children for living single living. Love requires changing whatever needs to be changed in our homes to salvage the short time left with your children.
11. Love empowers our children to be community- minded, assisting in areas of refinement and self-determination for their people

first, and then society.
12. Mothers need to be prayerful and careful how they rear their sons. The mother-son bond is more than biological. It is psychological too.
13. It is true that fathers have a role in helping sons become men, but mothers make 'gentlemen.'
14. A mother takes the lead with her son, especially during those nurturing years. She establishes the mental-emotional stability of the male-child more than the father does.
15. One of the greatest gifts a father can give to his son is to love his son's mother, or if they are not together, at least, be his mother's friend.
16. The mother-son relationship will most definitely have an immediate effect on the son living single.
17. So many children are bitter to this day because their parents made choices for them and enforced their will upon them to accomplish their self-serving agenda.
18. The habits of living single persist in adulthood, marriage and family unless these cultivated tendencies are addressed and resolved.
19. A major determinant in living single is knowing their purpose in life.
20. When parents empower their children with a balanced appreciation of themselves and their purpose, their reason for being, it counters identity-confusion and minimizes cultivating negative habits.
21. Children should not leave the side of their parents and cleave to living single until they have developed internal and external necessities. Good character, discipline and talents are internal qualities. Skills, expertise (profession and vocation) and economic independence are acquired external necessities.
22. There is a confidence, a stability and an optimism that accompanies that son or daughter who is ready. Parents can rest at night, virtually assured that their son or daughter is 'alright.'

23. Though no parent can predict the final outcome, children benefit by their staying by their parent's side until their character and career (purpose in life) has been established. They're ready for living single.

LABAN'S PLACE
5

"Then Jacob continued on his journey. He came to the land of the people of the East. He looked and saw a well in the field. Three flocks of sheep were lying nearby, because they drank water from this well. A large stone covered the mouth of the well. All the flocks would gather there. The shepherds would roll the stone away from the well and water the sheep. Then they would put the stone back in place. Jacob said to the shepherds there, 'My brothers, where are you from?' They answered, 'We are from Haran.' Then Jacob asked, 'Do you know Laban the grandson of Nahor?' They answered, 'We know him.' Then Jacob asked, 'How is he?' They answered, 'He is well. Look, his daughter Rachel is coming now with his sheep.' Then Jacob saw Laban's daughter Rachel and Laban's sheep. So he went to the well and rolled the stone from its mouth. Then he watered Laban's sheep. Now Laban was the brother of Rebekah, Jacob's mother. Then Jacob kissed Rachel and cried. He told her that he was from her father's family. He said that he was the son of Rebekah. So Rachel ran home and told her father. When Laban heard the news about his sister's son Jacob, Laban ran to meet him. Laban hugged him and kissed him and brought him to his house. Jacob told Laban everything that had happened. Then Laban said, 'You are my own flesh and blood' (Genesis 29:1-6; 10-14 NCV)."

Some of you remember growing up, when a girl got pregnant or the boy got in trouble, they were sent to a relative in another state-usually down south. This was the extended family that African people in America could call on, and they would be willing to help out. This valuable support system still exists today. When things get too challenging for a son or daughter, or a niece or nephew, some parents believed a change of environment might 'slow their roll.' There was no guarantee of the outcome, though more often than not, things turned out alright. But every now and then, a young person was sent out of the "frying pan into the fire," and came back home with some habits they didn't have before they left!

Jacob wasn't ready for living single, but he hardly had a choice in the matter after what he and his mother had done! Rebekah threw a few goat-skin shirts in his suitcase and Jacob was out of there! He finally arrived at Laban's place. Uncle Laban welcomes Jacob with open arms. What Jacob didn't know was that Uncle Laban was a con man! Let's be honest. Some of our relatives are not always on the up-and-up. Some of us have self-indulgent, jealous, lying, scheming relatives! We see them at our family reunions loud, drunk and argumentative. Most of their children stay in trouble or are out of control. It seems as if chaos and controversy 'wires' them. They always got some mess going on! Laban was one of those kind of relatives. He was always looking for an opportunity to use someone for his own benefit, even his own relatives. Unbeknown to him, Jacob would be his next victim.

Jacob wasn't prepared for single living and he certainly wasn't prepared for his uncle Laban! When you read Jacob's experiences at Laban's place (Genesis chapters 29-31), you will see that Jacob and his uncle Laban didn't get along. They ran con games on each other the whole twenty years Jacob lived at Laban's place!

Commentary

Because Jacob was not prepared by his parents for single living, he was not prepared for the challenging encounters with people outside of the home. Not only must we teach our children to be courteous and respectful, we must also teach them to be discerning. The multiplicity of negative attitudes and encounters out there can discourage a child or youth if the parents don't take the opportunity to make 'teachable moments' out of these jolting experiences with people.

For example, my family was watching the popular t.v. sitcom, 'In The House.' In this particular episode, the daughter wanted her mother to lie for her and tell a young male suitor she wasn't home while she hid another male admirer in the kitchen. I made note of that incident and my two daughters and I had a short discussion about it. We talked about the issue of lying and some of the consequences that follow, such as, children losing respect for their parents, violating people's trust in them, and being embarrassed when the truth is found out, etc. I encouraged them to always tell the truth in spite of the consequences. Honesty is the best choice.

My wife and I also use day-to-day experiences our daughters have in school- the teacher does something they believe is not appropriate; petty disagreements; jealous classmates; students who play unfair and cheat; and a host of other situations for discussion. We want them to gain insight and learn how to take the 'high road,' while preserving their integrity when encountering negative individual experiences. Though the experiences vary, learning how to respond appropriately benefits them immensely. The maxim I teach them is: "**Second response is better than first reaction.**" I made that up myself. It is better to take a moment to think before responding, than just to react first and have to apologize later.

The final point I want to make is the importance of instilling in our children an appreciation for family first. This might be easier said than done, depending upon your family matters. But the family should be the most affirming, encouraging, unifying entity on earth. In my home, we call it Harmony. Like instruments, tuned and skillfully played, harmony in the home gives children stability in their lives. Children find security in stability. When parents are not stable in the home, children are not secure, because they find their security in stability. When there is no harmony in the family, children are not secure, no matter how much your home alarm system cost.

There was no stability in Jacob's family- on his father's or mother's side. Now at Laban's place, Jacob will encounter more family challenges. Jacob is to discover the truth of the African proverb: "You don't just marry a person, you marry a family!"

Statements of Reflection on Chapter 5:
1. Not only must we teach our children to be courteous and respectful, we must also teach them to be discerning. The multiplicity of negative attitudes and encounters out there can discourage a child or youth if parents don't take the opportunity to make 'teachable moments' out of these jolting experiences with people.
2. Second response is better than first reaction. It is better to think before responding, than just to react first and have to apologize.
3. I encourage them (children) to always tell the truth in spite of the consequences. Honesty is the best choice.
4. It is important to instill in our children an appreciation for 'family first.'
5. The family should be the most affirming, encouraging, unified entity on earth.
6. When parents are not stable in the home, children are not secure, because they find their security in stability. When there is not harmony in the family, children are not secure, no matter how much your home alarm system costs.
7. "You don't just marry a person, you marry a whole family!"

SISTER, SISTER
6

"Then Laban said to Jacob, "You are my relative. But it is not right for you to keep on working for me without pay. What would you like me to pay you?' Now Laban had two daughters. The older was Leah, and the younger was Rachel. Leah had weak eyes, but Rachel was very beautiful. Jacob loved Rachel. So he said to Laban, 'Let me marry your younger daughter Rachel. If you will, I will work seven years for you.' Laban said, 'It would be better for her to marry you than someone else. So stay here with me.' So Jacob worked for Laban seven years so he could marry Rachel. But they seemed to him like just a few days. This was because he loved Rachel very much. After seven years Jacob said to Laban, 'Give me Rachel so that I may marry her. The time I promised to work for you is over.' So Laban gave a feast for all the people there. That evening Laban brought his daughter Leah to Jacob. Jacob and Leah had sexual relations together. In the morning Jacob saw that he had sexual relations with Leah! He said to Laban, 'What have you done to me? I worked hard for you so that I could marry Rachel! Why did you trick Laban said, 'In our country we do not allow the younger daughter to marry before the older daughter. But complete the full week of the marriage ceremony with Leah. I will give you Rachel to marry also. But you must serve me another seven years.' So Jacob did this and completed the week with Leah. (Laban gave his servant girl Zilpah to his daughter Leah to be her servant.) Then Laban gave Jacob his daughter Rachel as a wife. (Laban gave his servant girl Bilhah to his daughter Rachel to be her servant.) So Jacob had sexual relations with Rachel also. And Jacob loved Rachel more than Leah. Jacob worked for Laban another seven years (Genesis 29:15-30/NCV)"

What a way for Jacob to start a family! The deceiver of his own daddy and brother is deceived by his uncle Laban! What goes around comes around. This is a law of life. None of us can escape it. We reap what has been sown. It probably wasn't until Laban's deception with his daughters that Jacob realized the full magnitude of the faulty choices and decisions of his past. We can run from our past but we can't hide! Sooner or later, the chickens (family matters) do come home to roost!

As individuals, we reap the consequences of choices that were made **for** us and choices that were made **by** us. Usually the choices made for us have a lot to do with the choices made by us. I'll focus on that in the next chapter. Many children and youths (as well as adults) are reaping the consequences of decisions made for them by parents or other people. The faulty choices of Abraham and Isaac undoubtedly affected Jacob. That's how far-reaching the results of parents and people who violate natural or divine principles are. Remember the scripture I quoted earlier: "Visiting the consequences of the father upon the children, unto the third and fourth generation..." No one does anything that does not affect someone else. If parents would take into account the far-reaching effects of our choices and decisions- especially since the results will certainly affect our children and grandchildren; out of love, we would probably make better choices and decisions.

Then, there are faulty seeds sown by us, as individuals. The choices and decisions during our youth can and do affect our individual, marital and family matters! I heard a true story about a man who's two-year old daughter went blind. He took her to the physician and the physician asked him did anything get in her eyes. The man said no. After a thorough examination, the physician asked the man to think back when he was a youth. The man said, "When I was a young man, I did contracted a sexually transmitted disease. The physician concluded that was the cause. It was a tearful daddy who tucked his two-year old daughter in bed that night, wetting her blanket with his tears. The 'bills' came back, but someone he loved payed! Only then, do we wish we had chosen otherwise.

Laban was dead-wrong for doing what he did to Jacob. Nobody should to be mistreated, no matter what they have done. Two wrongs don't make it right. But with every cause, there is an effect. This is a law of life that cannot be revoked. In nature, whatever seed is sown, that is the kind of crop that will grow. Likewise, planting seeds for character, we reap what we sow. Jacob's mother sowed deception; Jacob became a deceiver. Jacob cultivated deception growing up, now he is reaping deception as a man. Jacob the 'fox' is out-foxed by his uncle Laban!

Jacob ends up marrying two twisted sisters, Leah and Rachel. As a boy, I tried to figure out how Laban pulled off sending in Leah without Jacob knowing. Was Jacob drunk? The scriptures does not say. The only conclusion I came to was that Laban had planned this with Leah and Rachel. Rachel was dressed in wedding garb and was with Jacob during the wedding festivities. Then at night, when it was dark and Jacob was waiting in the tent, Laban sent Leah in and they consummated the marriage just as Laban had planned. He knew Jacob and Rachel loved each other and that Jacob would probably agree to work seven more years for Rachel.

This makes me wonder what kind of home Laban and Rebekah, Jacob's mother, were brought up in? Were they the 'Bonnie and Clyde' of their community? It also makes me wonder what kind of home Leah and Rachel were reared in with a father like Laban. Laban didn't care if Jacob and Rachel loved each other. Only what Laban wanted mattered. Rachel, to whatever degree, had to go along with her father's devious plot. It hurt her and damaged (further) her relationship with her father and sister. Leah probably had a sinister smile on her face, knowing that she, and not Rachel, would have Jacob first. Can you imagine the family matters that would eventually surface in Jacob's home? Like I said, Jacob ran out of the frying pan into the fire!

The antagonism between Jacob and Laban only intensified after that infamous incident. Jacob worked as a shepherd, taking care of Laban's flock. But he was also stealing and amassing his own flock and herd on the side. What started out as a job for Jacob turned into fierce, almost violent competition. This went on for fourteen years! (Genesis 30:25-43).

But my greater concern is with Laban's daughters. A father must be very conscientious, rearing his daughter. How should a father treat his daughter? Like he holds a new born. He must be gentle, alert, careful, attentive, thoughtful, prepared and expectant. These are just a few fatherly characteristics I am learning. Laban was just the opposite, and Sister, Sister suffers the consequences.

Commentary

Sister, Sister is a delicate balancing act. The responsibility rests with parents to make the relationship between sisters (siblings) a win-win situation. I know because my wife and I have two daughters; a year and-a-half apart in age. **The difference between harmony or rivalry between Sister, Sister is how parents respond to and address sibling challenges.**

Sister, Sister will not always see eye-to-eye, and they don't have to. Sister, Sister will want their own way at times, so do adults. Sister, Sister will get upset with each other once in a while. That's nothing new in families. **The key to Sister, Sister relationships is for parents to be loving, fair, respectful, consistent and accepting of their individuality-** in that order. A double standard will not work. Comparing sister with sister is ill-advised. Even if one sister is more cooperative than the other, parents must not gravitate toward the one who cooperates and vilify the non-compliant sister. The preferential treatment Leah received is fodder for sibling rivalry. This rivalry explodes in their Sister, Sister marriage to Jacob.

Father-Daughter Relationship

One of the most powerful experiences in my life was to participate in the Million Man March on Washington, D.C., envisioned by Minister Louis Farrakan, Benjamin Chavis, and a host of grassroots Africans in America. All the paranoid African male naysayers missed being a part of incomparable history. Some positive opportunities come only once in life. He or she who hesitates is lost, as the adage goes. This is also true for a father who has daughters. We only get one opportunity to assist them in establishing a healthy concept of themselves, of family, of life and men. That is during childhood. There is no second childhood.

The mainstream media did everything they could to tarnish the impact of the Million Man March and continue to do so, but they can't take the truth away from me. I was there! What the mainstream conservative media won't report is the thousands of brothers who have called social service agencies, former wives or their child's mother after the March and recommitted themselves to paying alimony, child support, and take responsibility as a man and father. Many African men are getting involved in the lives of their children again and doing right by them. There are hundreds of Million Man March Local Organizing Committees who are involved and productive in the urban community!

The Million Man March inspired African men to acknowledge, address and resolve family matters. The Million Man March proves it's never too late for fathers to reconcile and begin the healing process. But it is more difficult to recover a relationship with his children later in life. Sometimes, the child will reject him for not being there when he/she really needed him. I believe father-daughter bonding is more difficult later in life.

Fathers establishing a wholesome, loving relationship with their daughters from birth is of utmost importance. Girls need their fathers to gain a proper concept of manhood first-hand. They need him to be a spiritual, moral, wise, patient guide in her life. A father doesn't have to be perfect to be principled. If our daughters have that, they have a jump on life, especially in relationships with men later in life. More often than not, a daughter may associate herself in dating and marriage with the kind of man her father is. Some statistics bear this out. It does not happen all the time, but it does happen more often than is reported.

When I was dating my wife, the first thing I did (when I visited her home in Philly) was to seriously observe her relationship with her father. I believed how she treats her father is how she would probably treat me. I also believe what she thinks about her father is the foundation of what she thinks about me in particular and men in general. I had conversations with her about him and with him about her. I needed to hear, see and understand what kind of man and father he was. This would help me, in part, to understand what kind of woman she was. I was satisfied. But you better believe, he was a factor in my total assessment of my relationship with his daughter.

The father-daughter relationship is a super-sensitive issue. When I articulate on the father-daughter relationship, some females get offended because they didn't have a father in the home. Let me share an experience with you. I was asked to be part of a panel discussion dealing with male-female relationships among Africans in America. The panel was diverse, consisting of singles, divorcees, widows, the engaged and married people (myself included). One young lady in the audience asked me, "What did you look for when you were dating your wife." My first replay was, "One of the first things I looked to see was how her relationship was with her father." I went on to qualify my statement by saying, "Fathers, to a great extent, teach their daughters how to love and respect men. How she treats her father is how she will probably treat me. The father is a girl's first point of reference in her conception of manhood." I also said, "A female could learn how to love and respect men and have a stable relationship but there is an added advantage when she has a good father growing up."

The young lady who asked the question got upset with me. Two years later, she finally confessed to me she was angry with me because she didn't grow up with a father in the home and I made it seem as if she did not know how to love or treat men unless she had a father in the home. I responded to her by saying I was sorry she misunderstood me. My emphasis was on the way she phrased the question: "What did YOU look for..." That's one of the first things I looked for. I did not try to make it the criteria for anyone else that day. But I don't apologize for it either. In fact, I'm glad I did and I made an excellent choice for a wife. I will tell the world that my wife's father, who is a deeply spiritual and principled man had a whole lot to do with the woman she is today!

The father-daughter relationship is something to be considered in dating and marriage. It doesn't have to be the deciding factor, but an honest consideration. Understanding the thoughts and views of a female concerning men is important. If she didn't get a healthy concept of manhood from her father or a positive male influence in her upbringing, it is important for a male admirer of her to know how she thinks concerning men and how her thought processes evolved to what they are at this time in her life. She can develop a healthy and balanced view of manhood without a father in the home, but she can't develop it without some positive male influence in her life at some time in her development- even if it was from reading the biographies of strong, principled, compassionate, women-respecting men. She has to have envisioned this kind of man, in some way, before it can be a part of her reality and her life.

Too often it is surmised that the father-son, mother-daughter relationship covers all bases. I don't think that's totally accurate. I believe and have experienced in most cases, it works just the opposite. It's the mother-son, father-daughter relationships that shape their child's concept of relationships with the opposite sex. It was my mother who taught me how to respect and love African women in a principled way. It was her as a person, her lifestyle and all her other attributes, too numerable to mention, that gave me a good foundational concept of African womanhood, even when I was living single.

Here's one reason why I believe the father-daughter relationship impacts so greatly. The nonspiritual male has a 'conquest mentality' as it relates to females. Growing up in the community, it was difficult to get a positive perspective on females, and I understood why. This patriarchal, chauvinistic, society inebriates a male psyche with the inferiority of females. As this pervasive 'learned behavior' from society at-large filters down to the 'streets,' many males think their identity resides in how many females they have conquered. (There was a lot of lying going on then!)

Generally speaking, I didn't hear many males speak in the positives about females. It was usually from a distorted concept of womanhood. Just listen to some of the lyrics by some popular musicians, or look at the 'rolling stone' lifestyles of well-know male actors to see how this distorted concept continues. Some musicians and actors don't corner this market only. Listen to leading national politicians. They second-class women in much of their rhetoric, policy positions and legislation. A similar message trumpets from most church pulpits by male-dominated leadership, as well as from the boardroom of multinational corporations.

This male-dominated society continues to demonstrate its difficulty in showing their sons the love and respect due all females. A father does give his son 'his' perspective on females and I don't minimize his influence on his son. But I believe, a father's special offering is the legacy he gives his daughter, the progenitor of the male-child, the mother and molder of the male species. It was awestruck to read the influence of Nero's mother on him! I was amazed to watch Connie Chung's interview with Newt Gingrich's mother and the influence she had on him! Fathers shape daughters; mothers shape their sons. (A few of you might disagree, but hear me out.)

My mother had more influence on me and my brother's thought processes than my father did. But my father had more influence on my sisters and their thought processes than my mother did. There are things only a mother can share with her son that gives him valuable insight into women. A father has his limitations with his son concerning the intricacies of women. My mother gave me an advantage through example and relationship with me as a boy, and now as a man.

Conversely, fathers have an advantage with their daughters. A female may tell my daughters how she thinks a man is, but I can show my daughters through example and relationship how a man is to be. Not only do they get the grand opportunity to see by example how I treat their mother, they also get the once in a lifetime privilege of having a positive male-female relationship with me. I am my daughters' first male relationship. This experience cannot be told to them. It is an experience that either a daughter gets or she doesn't get. This experience cannot be substituted by a mother-daughter relationship, though valuable as it is. I am the foundation of my daughter's male-female relationships for her individual, marital and family life. A whole lot is riding on my tires!

The father-daughter relationship becomes 'one' in a positive male-female relationship, long before the husband and wife become 'one' in the marital relationship. The father-daughter relationship has volumes to do with male-female relationships. When fathers treat their daughters with unconditional love and respect, while affirming their individuality, Sister, Sister learns to appreciate and discern men who love and respect them, and are not threatened by her individuality. As the father has helped them become secure in themselves, it's a take it or leave it deal with a man. Either a man accepts her for who she is and what she aspires to be or there will be some other man (who's mother has instilled discerning qualities and principles in him) who will.

Spiritual, self-respecting and secure daughters are not manipulated or moved as pawns on the masculine chessboard of life. They continue to find the good in men when they have encountered not-so-good men. They know there are still good men, and they don't judge all men by a few disrespectful men. Their father-daughter relationship is the reason for their healthy, balanced concept of manhood.

In my analysis, Laban blew it in his father-daughter relationship with Leah and Rachel! Laban fueled sibling rivalry between his daughters. They learned to be as devious and self-centered as their father. They were setup and used by a man to achieve their father's objective. Instead of the pedestal that women should be placed on, they became Laban's footstool! **Laban robbed his daughters of a most important essential at the most important time in their developing years: A loving, spiritual, principled father!**

It's the third generation from Abraham, and Jacob has a family now. The third and fourth generation from Abraham. None of their family matters have been resolved. They've only continued to perpetuate generation after generation. Most parents parent like their parents.

Statements of Reflection on Chapter 6:
1. What goes around comes around. This is a law of life. None of us can escape it. We reap what has been sown.
2. As individuals, we reap the consequences of choices that were made **for** us and choices that were made **by** us. Usually the choices made for us have a lot to do with the choices made by us.
3. Many children and youth (and adults) are reaping the consequences of decisions made for them by parents or other people.
4. No one does anything that does not affect someone else. If parents would take into account the far-reaching effects of our choices and decisions, especially as they will certainly affect our children and grandchildren; out of love, we would probably make better choices and decisions.
5. Choices and decisions as youth can and do affect our individual, marital and family life.
6. A father must be very conscientious rearing his daughter. How should a father treat his daughter? Like he holds a new born. He must be gentle, alert, careful, pay attention to, thoughtful, prepared and expectant.
7. The difference between harmony or rivalry between siblings is how parents respond to and address sibling challenges.
8. The key to sibling relationships is for parents to be loving, fair, respectful, consistent and accepting of their individuality.
9. Some opportunities come once in a lifetime. We only get one opportunity to assist daughters in establishing a healthy concept of themselves, of family, of life and men. That is during childhood.

UNDER ONE ROOF
7

"Yahweh saw that Jacob loved Rachel more than Leah. So Yahweh made it possible for Leah to have children, but Rachel didn't have any children. Leah became pregnant and gave birth to a son. She named him Reuben, because she said, 'Yahweh has seen my troubles. Surely now my husband will love me.' Leah became pregnant again and gave birth to another son. She named him Simeon. She said, 'Yahweh has heard that I am not loved. So Yahweh gave me this son.' Leah became pregnant again and gave birth to another son. She named him Levi. Leah said, 'Now, surely my husband will be close to me. I have given him three sons.' Then Leah gave birth to another son. She named him Judah. Leah named him this because she said, 'Now I will praise Yahweh.' Then Leah stopped having children. Rachel saw that she was not giving birth to children for Jacob. So she envied her sister Leah. Rachel said to Jacob, 'Give me children, or I'll die!' Jacob became angry with her. He said, 'Can I do what only Yahweh can do? Yahweh is the one who has kept you from having children.' Then Rachel said, 'Here is my servant girl Bilhah. Have sexual relations with her so she can give birth to a child for me. Then I can have my own family through her.' So Rachel gave Bilhah, her servant girl to Jacob as a wife. And he had sexual relations with her. She became pregnant and gave Jacob a son. Rachel said, 'Yahweh has declared me innocent. Yahweh has listened to my prayer and has given me a son.' So Rachel named this son Dan.

Bilhah became pregnant again and gave Jacob a second son. Rachel said, 'I have struggled hard with my sister, and I have won!' So Rachel named this son Naphtali. Leah saw that she had stopped having children. So she gave her servant girl Zilpah to Jacob as a wife. Then Zilpah had a son. Leah said, 'I am lucky.' So she named her son Gad. Zilpah gave birth to another son. Leah said, 'I am very happy! Now women will call me happy.' So she named that son Asher.

During the wheat harvest, Reuben went into the field and found some mandrake plants. (This was a plant that was believed to cause a woman to become pregnant). He brought them to his mother Leah. But Rachel said to Leah, 'Please give me some of your son's mandrakes.' Leah answered, 'You have already taken away my husband. Now you are trying to take away my son's mandrakes.' But Rachel answered, 'If you will give me your son's mandrakes, you may sleep with Jacob tonight.' When Jacob came in from the field that night, Leah went out to meet him. She said, 'You will have sexual relations with me tonight. I have paid for you with my son's mandrakes.' So Jacob slept with her that night. Then Yahweh answered Leah's prayer, and she became pregnant again. She gave birth to a fifth son. Leah said, 'Yahweh has given me what I deserve, because I gave my servant girl to my husband.' So Leah named her son Issachar. Leah became pregnant again, and gave birth to a sixth son. She said, 'Yahweh has given me a fine gift. Now surely Jacob will honor me, because I have given him six sons.' So Leah named the son Zebulun. Later Leah gave birth to a daughter. She named her Dinah. Then Yahweh remembered Rachel and answered her prayer. Yahweh made it possible for her to have children. She became pregnant and gave birth to a son. She said, 'Yahweh has taken away my shame.' She named him Joseph. Rachel said, 'I wish Yahweh would give me another son' (Genesis 29:31-35; 30:1-22 NCV).''

And some of you watch the Young and the Restless? Jacob's family matters are mind-boggling! I don't know how you felt as you read this story, but I marveled at all the baggage that was brought into one home, Jacob's home! It's more than a challenge to have two women (wives) living in the same home, married to the same man. There certainly will be some interesting dynamics going on there, to say the least! But when you add to that, a man who has fathered 12 children by four different women, all of them living together, that's incredible! I know Jacob's family was the talk of the community!

Leah bore Jacob four sons. What is so apparent was Leah's obsession to be loved and prioritized by Jacob. She thought bearing children for Jacob was the means to this end. Rachel had Jacob's love but didn't have his child. She encouraged Jacob into an extramarital liaison with her maid to compensate for her biological and emotional inadequacies. That's exactly what Jacob's grandparents, Abraham and Sarah did in a similar situation. Jacob exhibited the same moral and sexual weaknesses his grandfather Abraham displayed. Jacob had two sons by Bilhah. (He must have gone down to her tent again).

Like Rachel, Leah's servant is an extension of her insecurities and she offers Jacob her servant in hope of usurping Rachel's coveted position with Jacob. Sister Leah, goes tit-for-tat with Rachel, and sends her maid Zilpah in to Jacob, and Jacob consents again! Zilpah had two sons by Jacob. Then Leah has two more sons and a daughter by Jacob. Not long after, Rachel finally gives birth to a son. (She gives birth to another son named Benjamin later on but Rachel died while giving birth to him).

The pressure of getting married in most cultures is phenomenal. Marriage is an honored institution in any society. Marriage is the most spiritual, mental-emotional and socially affirming context for a man and woman to perpetuate humanity. Having children is another issue. The African proverb says, "Children are the reward of life." A home is empty without the music, the laughter, the innocence of children.

Sexual intercourse may produce children but it doesn't make parents; only parents make parents. The only way for parents to make parents (of their children) is to be a parent; not simply a biological parent, but a spiritual parent who lives according to the divine and natural principles of the Creator. This is the best point of reference a child can have to immolate when they become a parent. Isaac and Rebekah did not prepare Jacob for parenthood. Mr.

and Mrs. Laban did not prepare their daughters for parenthood. And the children were the chief recipients of their family matters.

What About The Children?

I feel sorry for Jacob's children. Their challenge was not being born into a large family. I know parents with large families who have produced outstanding children. I'm referring to the conditions the children have to live in that were created by their parents. When the happiness of the parent is more important than the mental-emotional health of their children, something is terribly wrong with Parenthood. Consider these quotations:

Mothers Feelings Mold Disposition of Unborn Child: "The thoughts and feelings of the mother will have a powerful influence upon the legacy she gives her child. If she allows her mind to dwell upon her own feelings, if she indulges in selfishness, if she is peevish and exacting, the disposition of her child will testify to the fact. Thus many have received as a birthright almost unconquerable tendencies to evil. If the mother unswervingly adheres to righteous principles, if she is temperate and self-denying, if she is kind, gentle, and unselfish, she may give her child these same precious traits of character."

Insatiable Craving, Unholy Desires Transmitted to Young: "Both parents transmit their own characteristics, (mental and physical) as well as their dispositions and appetites to their children. Liquor drinkers and tobacco users may, and do, transmit their insatiable craving, their inflamed blood and irritable nerves, to their children. The licentious often bequeath their unholy desires, and even loathsome diseases, as a legacy to their offspring."

Parents Provide Child's Life Equipment: "What the parents are, that to a great extent the children will be. The physical conditions of the parents, their dispositions and appetites, their mental and moral tendencies, are to a greater or lesser degree reproduced in their children."

Parents May Have Transmitted To Their Children Tendencies: "If the appetite for unhealthy food and for stimulants and narcotics has been transmitted to them as a legacy from their parents, what a fearfully solemn responsibility rests upon the parents to counteract negative traits which they have given to their children! How earnestly and diligently should the parents work to do their duty, in faith and hope, to their unfortunate offspring."

Parenthood is the highest of responsibilities! It is through parenthood that family matters perpetuate. The wholistic health and well-being of the family largely rests with parenthood. Am I blaming parents? It's not about blaming but about transmission. I believe a 'source' must be identified if solutions and resolutions are to come about. How can anyone give solutions if she or he has not pinpointed the source? **The central consideration of this book identifies the source as: Unrecognized or unresolved inherited and cultivated traits.** These traits, sooner or later, surface in our individual, marital and family life, impeding balanced character development and wholesome relationships.

I read botanist Gregor Mendel's work in cross-breeding plants. I also reviewed the process of conception, as it relates to the genes and chromosomes. Here's what fascinated me. In spite of millions of sperm cells, only one successfully fertilizes the female egg. Yet, in that one sperm is the father's genetic family history. In the nuclei of the female's egg is the mother's genetic family history. Traditional African culture recognizes not simply two individuals that marry but two families! The children become the recipient of both family histories! It all has to do with Parenthood.

Some of you can't figure out what happened because your marriage started out so good! But what you didn't know anything about, or you couldn't see laying dormant was inherited and cultivated tendencies of two families that were unrecognized or unresolved. In time, they surface through our character, personality, attitude, temperament, and even lifestyle! These traits sabotage relationships and exasperate family matters.

What inherited traits are predominant in your family? Are you struggling with tendencies that is common among your family? Are these traits generational, perpetuating from one generation to the next? Do you see any in your children? How about your grandchildren? There are traits parents pass on to their children that they can't whip out! What parents call some behavioral problems, are in reality, inherited and cultivated traits your children got from you! You can't spank or punish yourselves out of your child! You have to work it out at the source!

Daily, I get calls from parents about their children's drug problems. But some of these same parents couldn't keep a cigarette, shot glass, or 'joint' out of their hands when they were younger! Now, some of their children have the same problems! Although alcohol, cigarettes and drug use are individual choices, should some of their children choose to use them, they usually have a greater predisposition for having a serious addiction. This fact is medically substantiated.

In summation, there are internal and external determinants that exasperate family matters. Faulty inherited traits and our environment (society) are the internal and external factors, respectively. One is transferred to society and society transfers it back to the family.

The hope and healing begins with the African term Sankofa, which means: "We Must Return To The Source To Go Forward." Parenthood is a good source to return to in the recognition and resolution of family matters. We can understand Jacob better when we return to his source, his parents Isaac and Rebekah. We understand Isaac better when we know about his upbringing in the home of Abraham and Sarah. And we definitely understand how Sister, Sister (Leah and Rachel) resulted by seeing how they were brought up in Laban's place!

We must return to the source, not to blame or to make excuses for anyone, but for the purpose of identification and resolution; and then to go forward toward hope and healing.

Some of you saw serious warning lights flashing when you were dating or engaged, but you ignored them! Some of you spend time and energy blaming each other instead of identifying the source and seeking help. Others of you are more intent on changing their mates than changing yourself. Still others find it easier to bail out of your relationships than 'buck up' in the marriage. You can get out of as many marriages or relationships as you want but something will surely 'visit' the next one, and the next one, because all unrecognized or unresolved inherited or cultivated traits, sooner or later will find their way into that relationship. **Individual, marital and family matters can only be resolved at the source!**

What about the children? What about their children's children? This is what Jacob is about to tell to them as he lays on his death bed.

Statements of Reflection on Chapter 7:
1. Marriage is the most spiritual, mental-emotional and socially affirming context for a man and woman to perpetuate humanity.
2. "Children are the reward of life."
3. Sexual intercourse may produce children but it doesn't make parents; only parents make parents.
4. When the happiness of the parent is more important than the mental-emotional health of their children, something is terribly wrong with Parenthood.
5. Traditional African culture recognizes not simply two individuals that marry but two families! The children become the recipient of both family histories.
6. Parenthood is a good source to return to in the recognition and resolution of family matters.
7. We must return to the source, not to blame or to make excuses for anyone, but for the purpose of identification and resolution; and then to go forward toward hope and healing.
8. Individual, marital and family matters can only be resolved at the source!

ME AND THE BOYZ

8

"Then Jacob called for all his sons to come in and said to them, 'Come and gather around my bed, so I can tell you what Yahweh has told me about your future and the future of your descendants' (Genesis 49:1/ CWB)."

Before my daughters were born, my wife and I tried to imagine what kind of children they would be. Would they be kind and respectful? Would they have a good sense of humor? Would they be talented? What traits would we pass on to them? The most obvious inherited trait is physical characteristics. Most children look like their parents.

There are temperament that substantiate inherited traits passed from parent to child. Some temperament surface soon after birth. I've witnessed babies with tempers that rival any adult! Try to take a toy out of their hand and they will go ballistic! That temper is not learned behavior; that's inherited. Discerning parents notice temperament and traits they have passed on to their children. I see a few of my own in my daughters, however, they have my wife's positive traits to overshadow them.

As children of human parents, we have all been paid a visit! You know it! I know it! We know what character traits we got from our parents and what traits our children got from us! In parenthood, the inescapable reality is: "Visiting the consequences of the fathers upon the children." Consequences are not all negative. There are positive consequences too. These positive traits are the byproduct of positive choices, decisions and moral practices of the parents. A child 'catches' these traits from the parent.

What a joy it is to see positive character traits in children. All children have some positive character traits. They are to be developed. For example, a child inherits from his/her parent the ability to meet, befriend, and interact with people easily. If this positive trait is identified and developed, this child could do well in their own business or work in the public sector. It is important for parents to affirm and develop all positive character traits.

Conversely, we all have received a visit or two or three, of negative character traits from our grandparents or parents; and those of us who are parents, have passed on some to our children! These undeniable inherited traits impact negatively on the character development of children as they grow into youth and adulthood. There is no human who does not need some kind of healing intervention in their lives. My point is, all of us have inherited tendencies from our parents that need to be resolved. **If parents do not address negative inherited traits at the point of recognition, children will cultivate them.** Cultivated traits usually become a lifestyle or habit that is difficult to break.

Many of you have known parents who have recognized detrimental traits in their child but played it off as a 'phase' the child was going through. They figure the child would grow out of it as he or she got older. In reality, these traits must be 'rooted out' immediately and not permitted to develop.

Permit me to refer back to inherited temper that surfaces in some children. This should not be overlooked but dealt with each time it surfaces. This trait is not to be punished, but always addressed. The parent must speak to the baby at that time even though you might think the baby doesn't understand your words. You must register your disapproval in a gentle but firm voice. Then you must tell them the appropriate response when something doesn't go their way. You have to be consistent. Whenever the temper surfaces, address it. The child will learn to associate your corrective response with their action and in time understand.

This is your best deterrent against temper-cultivation until they are old enough for you to address it in more creative words and non-punishing object lessons.

Parents allow children to cultivate negative traits when they are ignored. Some parents think if they ignore them, they will fade away. Others think if they let the child 'carry on' and ignore negative responses, the child will realize the parent is not paying them any attention and will eventually stop. Maybe, maybe not. But ignoring negative traits or responses permit them to lie dormant within a child. The objective is not to ignore them but to resolve them by addressing all negative traits and responses at the point of recognition so they won't cultivate them to their detriment later in life.

It may take some time but it works. I know because my mother did not permit me to cultivate (in her home) traits that she recognized as negative. She "nipped it in the bud" as the old saying goes. I never cultivated a temper, a smart mouth, a rebellious spirit, or a myriad of attitudes or temperament because my mother did not permit me to. She firmly but lovingly dealt with it at the point of recognition. No weed can grow if it is not permitted to take root. The same applies to character.

Character development is like a garden. It can be constantly and joyfully attended to or blatantly neglected and ignored. Whatever parents sow, the children will reap. Jacob learned this all too painful lesson near the end of his life. Jacob's boyz ended up lying and deceiving him in his old age, just like Jacob had deceived his father Isaac in his old age! What goes around, comes around!

The personalities and characters of some of Jacob's children, though not all bad, reveal how inherited and cultivated traits can be passed on when they remain unrecognized or unresolved. Jacob calls his 12 sons to his bedside:

"**Reuben**, my first son, you are my strength. Your birth showed I could be a father. You have the highest position among my sons. But you are uncontrolled like water. So you will no longer lead your brothers. You had sexual relations with Bilhah, your brother's mother, on my bed. You dishonored me. The personality of your descendants will be just like yours- strong, but immoral.

"**Simeon and Levi**, you are instruments of cruelty! Your violent temper is a curse to you. You don't hesitate at the slightest provocation to get revenge. Your descendants will have the same personality as yours!

"**Judah**, you will be respected and praised. Your descendants will be leaders and kings. Someone from your family will always be on the throne and will rule until the real king comes; then the nations will obey Him.

"**Zebulun**, you love the ocean. Your descendants will live by the sea and be a welcomed haven for ships and a rest to weary travellers.

"**Issachar**, you are strong like a donkey. You work hard and enjoy it. You are industrious. Your descendants will be like you.

"**Dan**, you like to rule over people; your actions are as crafty as a snake. You're a backbiter. Your descendants will be just like that!

"**Gad**, you are peaceful, and an easy prey for people to take advantage of, but you will not be afraid to stand up to them. Your descendants will be like you.

"**Asher**, you like to farm and produce rich crops and provide for others; your descendants will like to do the same.

"**Naphtali**, you are graceful like a deer running free. You love the beauty of nature, works of art, and the flow of gracious words. Your descendants will be just like you.

"**Joseph**, you are like a fruitful vine. You also have a free spirit like a colt on a hillside. Your enemies will fiercely attack you but you will remain steady and strong. You are known to depend on the power of the Almighty to be with you. Yahweh will help you. Yahweh will bless you. May Yahweh bless your children forever.

"**Benjamin**, you are like a wolf who will to kill to sustain yourself. You will do anything to stay alive. Your descendants will be just like that."

Jacob slowly lays back on his bed, motioning them to leave. His past floods his mind. Tears roll from his blind eyes. Oh, for another chance!

Commentary

I have on my desk a booklet entitled, Tyranny Of The Urgent! The author quoted a factory manager who once said to him, "Your greatest danger is letting the urgent tasks crowd out the important." The author went on to say, "We live in constant tension between the urgent and the important. The problem is that many important tasks need not be done today, or even this week...these activities can wait a while longer. But urgent tasks call for immediate action. Their seemingly irresistible demands devour our energy. Yet with a sense of loss, we recall the important tasks that have been shunted aside. We realize that we've become slaves to the tyranny of the urgent." [10]

How sobering it is for parents to think back to their childhood or youth and see how our past reveals itself in our present and we realize that our character repeats itself in our children! But we still have hope! Still sparkling beneath the mire of painful family matters are the glitter of good that have shown through in our children and families. No person is all bad. There are redeeming virtues in all of us.

Though the negatives overshadow the positives, Yahweh made sure the positive inherited traits were not overlooked. Diamonds in the rough are still diamonds, waiting for someone to recognize its worth and work with it until it fulfills its ultimate purpose.

Likewise, our children need the same attention and work. The challenge is to start doing what is important instead of what is urgent; that is, recognizing and resolving the negative inherited and cultivated character traits. For this important task, we must secure hope and healing.

Statements of Reflection on Chapter 8:

1. How sobering it is for parents to think back to their childhood and youth and see how our past reveals itself in our present and we realize that our character repeats itself in our children!
2. There are temperament that substantiate inherited traits passed from parent to child.

3. Discerning parents notice temperament and traits they have passed on to their children.
4. Consequences (traits) are not all negative. There are positive traits that are the byproduct of positive choices, decisions and moral practices of parents. They are 'caught and taught' by the child from the parent.
5. There is no human who does not need some kind of healing intervention in their lives.
6. If parents do not address negative inherited traits at the point of recognition, children will cultivate them. Cultivated traits usually become a lifestyle or habit that is difficult to overcome.
7. Parents permit children to cultivate negative traits when they are ignored.
8. The objective is to resolve, not to ignore; to address all negative traits at the point of recognition so they won't cultivate them to their detriment later in life.
9. Character development is like a garden. it can be constantly and joyfully attended to or blatantly neglected and ignored.
10. "Your greatest danger is letting the urgent things crowd out the important."
11. Still sparkling beneath the mire of painful family matters are the glitter of good that have shown through in our children and families. No person is all bad. There are redeeming virtues in all of us.
12. Diamonds in the rough are still diamonds; waiting for someone to recognize its worth and work with it until it fulfills its ultimate purpose.
13. The challenge is to start doing what is important instead of what is urgent; that is, recognizing and resolving the negative inherited and cultivated character traits.

HOPE AND HEALING
9

"And Yahweh said to Jacob, 'It's time for you to go back home to the land of your ancestors, and I will be with you.' So Jacob sent word to Leah and Rachel to meet him in the field where he kept his flocks. He said to them, 'I've noticed your father has not been friendly to me as he use to be, but Yahweh has been with me. You know how hard I worked for your father, but he has cheated me. Over the past twenty years, he's changed my wages ten times. But Yahweh has been with me and kept me from harm' (Genesis 31:3-7)."

"In my dream, the Angel of Yahweh called, 'Jacob!' I answered, 'Here I am!' He said, 'I have noticed how Laban has been treating you...now it's time to go home, back to your own land and family.' Leah and Rachel said, 'There's nothing for us here. We have no inheritance or dowry coming, so why stay? In fact, our father treats us more like strangers than like daughters. He sold us to you as he sells property, and the money he made from you, he's already spent. Everything Yahweh has taken from our father and given to you is legitimately ours and belongs to us and to our children. So whatever Yahweh has told you to do, do it, and let's go.' As soon as they said this, Jacob made plans to leave. He packed and loaded his tents, put his wives and children on camels and headed for home. He tool all his herds with him and whatever else he had accumulated during is stay in Mesopotamia and headed back to his father Isaac who was still alive in the land of Canaan (Genesis 31:11-18 CWB)."

"You must return to the source to go forward." After 20 years of unabated family matters, Jacob is going home. **If there is a primary goal all individuals, marriages and families need to**

accomplish, it is healing. Healing cannot be accomplished without returning to the source. All unrecognized or unresolved inherited and cultivated traits can only be rooted out at its source.

But here's one of the biggest impediments to healing: Most grandparents and parents won't talk! They have key information that could unlock closets where family skeletons are hidden, but they won't say anything! The scriptures say we, "Perish for lack of knowledge (Hosea 4:6)." Many of our elders think they are keeping 'bad' information from us; what we don't know does hurt us!

Inherited and cultivated traits that surface generation after generation could come to a screeching halt in many families if those who know the source would open up. When families are hurting, true love does not keep silent. Grandparents, uncles, aunts, relatives or parents who know the 'source' of family matters must give their children (that includes adults) a point of reference. They must give adequate and complete information. We have to know the root, to understand the fruit! We must return to the source if we are to go forward!

Some family secrets are so horrible that many of our grandparents and parents don't want us to know anything about them. They think they are shielding us from abominable family secrets. In reality, these are the very secrets that usually surface again through our temperament, personality or lifestyle and we must be made aware of them.

A sobering African proverbs is: "When an elder dies, it's like the burning of a library!" Too many of our parents, grandparents, aunts and uncles are taking pertinent family knowledge to the grave! I'm talking about valuable information that is the key to unlocking the chains of negative traits that have been binding many of us or our family for years!

At least, Jacob called his boyz to his deathbed and let them know what their future would hold based on his past family matters! He did the honorable thing. Jacob probably shared more with them than the narrative reveals. Jacob's boyz could only understand their future by knowing the past.

Jacob's heartfelt talk with his boyz also says to me that no matter what situation we are in, that's not how we have to end up. When a defect in character is identified or brought to our attention, it is a call to resolving or remedying it, a summons to mastery over it.

Many of you are grown and you still don't know why you have done or continue to do some of the things you do, even though it has hurt your personal, marital or family relationships. But still, your parents know you are struggling with family matters and they still won't open their mouths.

I know some of you are already seeing traces of inherited and cultivated traits surfacing in some of your children and grandchildren. Family matters are surfacing earlier than ever before in children and they are having a more devastating effect on them than ever before.

Let me give you a few experiences to reinforce the need for returning to the source before healing can take place. The first is someone very close to me. For the sake of helping you resolve your family matters, I know you won't mind me sharing your experience.

When she was a very young girl, she was her father's 'lucky girl.' He took her with him to gamble. She played his hand in cards and won lots of money for her father. She developed an obsession for gambling and was good at it. As a teenager and adult, she gambled. Years later, she gave up gambling. But now she has a son who has inherited and cultivated her gambling obsession.

He is not responsible for what he inherited, nor is any child the blame for traits they inherited from parents. But he is accountable for his solution. For healing to take place, he must acknowledge he has a problem. Then he must seek to identify the 'source' of it. This is where his mother assists in his solution. She must give him that point of reference by telling him how his grandfather gambled and she had a gambling problem, and he has inherited this vice from them. With the appropriate intervention and a positive support system, he can completely overcome his gambling habit. But his mother has to talk and become involved in his healing. If she keeps her past a secret, her son's recovery may be prolonged.

The son not only is accountable for securing intervention and/or treatment for his problem, he has to talk to his children if he is to stop this vice from 'visiting' his own children. He has a great deal to do with "the buck stopping here." He cannot not lock this gambling 'skeleton' in a closet once he's overcome it. He must share this 'key' information with his children. As painful or embarrassing as it might be, self-disclosure is vital in inhibiting the perpetuation of gambling in his offspring.

He must even bring his mother in on the discussion with his children. He can't tell them, "Just say no!" He and his mother must share the ends and outs, the waste of time and money, even the dangers associated with gambling.

If he thinks his children don't need to know about his past gambling habit, he is mistaken and he's setting his children up! The reality of inherited traits is awesome. If inherited traits are cultivated by the children, it may take them a lifetime to recover! Clean all the skeletons out of the closet of your family! Beginning with the ones you recognize that are surfacing in the lives of your children. As the adage says, "To be forewarned is to be forearmed."

I want to share my personal experience to reinforce the need for elders and parents to tell their children the 'source' of family matters. I'm revealing a 'skeleton' that most people who know me never knew. I'm doing this because I am not in denial; nor will I hide my personal mistakes from anyone who needs hope and healing.

I believe I had one of the best childhood's any child could have. Our family didn't have much, but our needs were supplied. The rearing I received was spiritual, fun and principled. It wasn't until I graduated from high school that I changed directions. I started hanging out with nonspiritual and unprincipled people. They were not hardcore. They were more sociable- party people.

I started smoking reefer and cigarettes. And for the next four years, I don't think I passed up a drug that was out there!

Mescaline, window pane, blotter acid, LSD, syrup, angel dust, wacky weed, cocaine, snorting heroin, sopers, black beauties, Thunderbird, Mad Dog, Ripple, Boonesfarm, beer, you name it! I didn't turn down anything; not even my collar!

It was like I was in a dark cave with scales on my eyes and I could not see. I was lying, stealing, selling, strapping (carrying a gun), and working eight hours a day, making pretty good money.

In 1975 I got busted and believe me, the scales fell off my eyes. But I wasn't arrested as much as I was rescued! I know it was the prayers of my mother that I made it out of that cave, alive and into my right mind!

I shared this brief account for a reason. There are many children who have received a good, spiritual, principled upbringing with spiritual and principled parents, but do not know they have dormant inherited traits within. As long as they are not activated, they are not cultivated toward habits.

It wasn't until 1995 (twenty years later) that my mother told me something I never knew. She said that before my father 'joined the church,' he had a drinking problem! I never knew that. He was 'in the church' when I was born, so I never saw him, much less, knew he drank or smoked.

I want to make two points concerning my personal experience I just shared. Number one, spirituality is not inherited, it is acquired. Children don't inherit spirituality from their parents. That is an individual choice. Just because a parent is spiritual doesn't mean the child will automatically be born spiritual. Spirituality is not transferrable. Spirituality is a choice, not an endowment. That's something each person must choose for themselves. Even if parents are 'in the church' there is no guarantee that their children will not inherit their negative traits. In all likelihood, they will.

My second point is this: Children, whose parents indulge in drugs and alcohol (or whatever vice), have a greater predisposition to having that same problem. This is a medical fact. I never knew I had a greater chance of having a drug addiction than a child whose parents never indulged.

I am accountable for my choices and decisions and I made a conscious choice to use drugs. I'm not blaming my father. But when I activated that inherited tendency, I went the whole nine yards! It was like I couldn't stop! I could not figure out why I liked getting high so much. I used to boast that I would never stop getting high! I'd die before I stopped getting high! I'm just so thankful to the Creator and for the prayers of my parents that I stopped getting high before I died!

If my father had been open and willing to share his past with me, maybe I would have learned from his mistakes and would have never used drugs in the first place. But my father never talked. He never shared any of his past. His silence became part of my problem. His sharing could have been part of my solution. When my mother told me of his drinking problem twenty years later, I was silent, but somewhat dismayed that I didn't know years ago.

I'm going to get even more personal. I know that someone reading this book needs to hear this. So often we are told to keep our business in the family. That is often good advice. But when it comes to someone learning how to be healed, my love for people comes before hiding 'skeletons.'

While I am writing this book, my father is in a nursing home. He had a couple of strokes, he's on dialysis, has high blood pressure, and other health problems. Recently, I asked him some pertinent questions about his background, his upbringing; and other vital information so I can have a point of reference and know what to watch out for, especially for my daughters sake. But he wouldn't talk! I asked him what did his parents die from? What were the predominant health problems in his immediate family? What did his sisters die from? What were his 'family matters' growing up? He told me nothing.

I don't want my daughters to 'activate' inherited tendencies if they can be avoided because he chooses not to share critical information of his past! You better believe I told my daughters about my challenges with drugs! My concern is not their perception of me. If they have inherited a predisposition from me, I don't want them to activate it. They don't ever have to struggle with that problem if they honor my wisdom and instructions concerning the complete and adequate information I have given them.

When I lecture on this topic of family matters, many people talk with me afterwards and tell me their elders and parents won't talk either. That generation thinks they are 'protecting' us from something. That's not protection; that's presumption. And presumption can be fatal!

Inherited and cultivated traits are making casualties out of our lives, marriages and families! If elders, parents, or knowledgeable relatives don't give our families the 'source' of these challenges, many of us will never be healed! Inherited and cultivated traits will continue generationally like it did in the family of Abraham, Isaac and Jacob.

I know it's painful to have to tell our children that we did this and that, but we must never sacrifice our children's health and well-being just to keep a skeleton in the closet! To have any information that could contribute to the source and solution of any family matter and not share it is wrong. That kind of silence is a sin!

Why is returning to the source so essential to healing? We can't analyze the 'fruit' without understanding the 'root.' As it concerns healing, any physician worth her or his salt must have some knowledge of the 'source' (family history) if they are to make a prognosis that as lends to healing. If a physician is ignorant or deprived of essential knowledge of the root cause, a misdiagnosis can result.

This leads me to my third and final point. We need to know the 'source' of all our family health problems; especially those that continue generationally. This not only includes physical health but also mental-emotional health.

Most of you know physical maladies such as cancer, tumors, enlarged hearts, high blood pressure, strokes, etc., that have plagued your families. There is someone very close to me whose husband died from an enlarged heart at the age of 36. His father died from an enlarged heart! This young man could have lived if he would have been given the source and solution of this health problem in his family. He seemed so healthy until he was hospitalized. He found out too late.

If information assists in the diagnosis and prognosis of the patient, how much more should you or your children have a working knowledge of the health concerns on both sides of your family as early as possible! This pertinent knowledge may increase the longevity of your family.

When I asked my father if he has any knowledge of any of his parents or family members having similar health problems, he said he didn't know. Trying to find out health information on his side of the family is virtually impossible. Only one of his sisters is still alive. She told me what she could, but her knowledge of their parent's health status is limited.

If you are faced with limited knowledge of your family's health problem like I am, wisdom dictates that you become health-conscious. My wife and I are educating ourselves and our children for healthier living. This is a good way to prevent unnecessary health problem. Though it is possible to have health problems, it decreases self-initiated health problems when we practice healthy lifestyles and eat health foods in our family. This is a primary way for me to assist my daughters and their future children with little-to-no health information from my father's side of the family.

I also direct inquiring people at my lectures on family matters to read material that addresses a stress-free lifestyle and to a diet that encourages the balanced use and benefits of natural herbs and natural remedies; vegetarianism; and alternative medicine or naturopathy. This knowledge and practice can rebuild some damaged cells and restore the body naturally as best as possible (depending on the degree of damage done).

I do not advise them to stop taking chemical medicines without consulting a certified health professional. I do encourage them to research and examine a natural lifestyle. This is my best contribution for those whose relatives won't or don't open up about family related health concerns.

No child should suffer because of our silence, embarrassing as it may be. Elders and parents must divulge all information that assists in the solution to family matters. Imparting this legacy is more valuable than leaving them money and land. Without this knowledge that many of you have, they may not be around long enough to use it, or healthy enough to enjoy it.

Just as I have addressed the physical health of the family, mental health is equally as important in family matters. If we are honest, most of our families are not healthy mentally or emotionally. It is a challenge to stay mentally and emotionally healthy, especially in western society.

I guess this is as good a time to say it: I want to go on record and say that I believe that African people have their own unique set of mental health challenges that cannot be defined, categorized or solved by Eurocentric psychology or its modalities. I don't believe that the mental-emotional health of African people can be accurately and honestly diagnosed or defined by a Eurocentric construct which is itself, the 'source' of many of the mental-emotional and social problems of Africans in America.

The psycho-social consequences of the dominating white society unleashed upon the African family have been devastating beyond imagination. In modern history alone, 400 years of enslavement, rape, murder, colonization, Jim Crow, lynching, KKK, castration, Supreme Court rulings, segregation laws, redlining, untried murders, counterintelligence programs, sterilization programs, the Tuskegee experiment, inadequate housing and health services, assassinations, un/underemployment, unfair mandatory sentencing laws, bank loan rejections, and white supremacist social policies (just to name a few), reveal how much more psychologically and socially challenged Africans in America are!

Euro-Americans cannot fathom life with this kind of unabated inhumane treatment suffered by African people in America. Yet, so many of them are willingly silent (especially the white church) while these injustices escalate instead of decrease. All the while, the mainstream media blames the victim and shrewd politicians incite fears (play the race card) for reelection purposes.

In his insightful book, Chains and Images of Psychological Slavery, Dr. Na'im Akbar analyzes and synthesizes the lingering effects of the European dehumanization of Africans. This must-read book enlightens its readers to the horrific psychological scars that still affect the collective African psyche even today.[11] The internalization of this psycho-social assault plays itself out in many deleterious and destructive ways for many. It ranges from self-hatred and self-destruction to insanity. Some Africans in America also feel a need to identify or assimilate with someone other than their own people or culture.

Coupled with this psycho-social reality is the undeniable truth of European males who raped myriads of African women (or sent their sons in to violate them), yielding offspring who inherited and cultivated their traits. This 'source,' is entirely excluded from innumerable so-called scientific 'studies' done on the psycho-social condition of Africans in America.

The recovery of the mental-emotional health of African families is a complex issue. There are no easy answers. Contrary to all the rhetoric of the United States being a democracy, there is no real protection in the Constitution of the United States for Africans in America. (This increases stress and anxiety among Africans in America. These psychosomatic challenges affect the physical health of many Africans in America.)

Dr. Claude Anderson explains this truth: "The U.S. Constitution has historically been and continues to be an impediment to black political and economic empowerment and self-sufficiency. During the formative years of this nation, the Constitution outright excluded blacks from the privileges of citizenship, the acquisition of wealth and power, and the enjoyment of the fruits of their own labor. Moreover, the Constitution shackled blacks so that members of the majority white society and any other ethnic or racial group could use blacks for socioeconomic gains." [12]

Dr. Anderson goes on to note that this same Constitution is now being used by conservative entities to block any effort by Africans in America to seek justice and remedy past and present discrimination. These efforts to right wrongs are labeled as reverse discrimination and unconstitutional.

Contrary to popular belief, the American educational system cannot the answer the mental-emotional challenges facing Africans in America. The American educational system has an undeniable history as one of the leading culprits of the so-called psycho-social inferiority of African people.

Some renowned Euro-American educators have, in the past, and continue to theorize that African people have an inferior intellect to whites. They believe whites have a superior intellect. Both are said to be inherent in the genes. This so-called inferior-superior intellect is passed on genetically to their children.

If these theories on intellect are to be proven true, there is one question that remains to be answered: Which is the Original Race, The Caucasian or The African? This question was posed by four African psychologist, Drs. Na'im Akbar, Wade Nobles, Cedric X (Clarke), and D. Phillip McGee, in their book, Voodoo Or IQ: An Introduction to African Psychology. This is their reply:

"Many Euro-American psychologist, no doubt, would consider this question a theological one at best and irrelevant at worse. Such apparent unconcern with questions of origin is rather peculiar, given the great current concern with the role of genetic factors in human behavior. Clearly, if one is to be consistent with any genetic thesis, one must surely give at least nominal attention to the nature of the first human gene pool - for it is from this original gene pool that all contemporary genes were derived.

If, then, we are to be concerned about the genetic transmission of human intelligence, we must admit only one of two possibilities: either the white race is evolutionary prior to the black, in which case whatever intelligence (or lack thereof) blacks have has been inherited from whites; or the black race is evolutionary prior to white, in which case the reverse would be true."[13]

Simply translated, if whites are the original people then the so-called inferior intellect Africans are accused of possessing was given to them by whites. If Africans are the original people, then the so-called superior intellect of whites was passed to them from Africans.

It is necessary for me to raise this issue that you might understand the mental-emotional challenges, especially among Africans in America, that have 'sources' other than just their own selves.

All unrecognized or unresolved mental-emotional challenges, whatever the source, sooner or later, surface in some degree, in individual, marital or family matters. Africans in America must ascertain the degree of inferiority they have internalized and access how it negatively affects their individual, marital and family relationships. All sources must be identified, defined, addressed and resolved by Africans in America with the assistance of those who are qualified and gifted to provide mental-emotional stability, hope and healing.

If you have read between the lines, you have discerned another unfortunate but true reality peeking through. That is the acquired traits that many Euro-Americans have inherited and cultivated from their elders and parents! The superiority claim over all others in the human family is a denial of the truth and a sickness within itself. It is indicative of unrecognized or unresolved 'skeletons' that have surfaced in their individual, marital and family matters. Sigmund Freud can't solve this one. In fact, he inherited this sickness himself.

For white supremacy and its brutal inhumanity to operate unabated, generation after generation, denotes a serious transference! To refuse to acknowledge people of color's humanity and practice injustice is a mental health problem!

The war on people of color continues worldwide. The World Bank's austerity measures create debtor nations. The C.I.A. deposes democratically elected leaders, and multinational corporations continue to rob Africa of its natural resources in the midst of rampant starvation and poverty. In the U.S., this 'war' continues with the stroke of Bill Clinton's pen. One million more children (along with their families) were signed into poverty for political expediency, in the guise of the Welfare Reform Bill. What about the children? The 'war' on children is a mental health problem!

Worse is that this ideology and behavior has continued generation after generation among many Europeans worldwide! This collective mindset undoubtedly has been inherited and cultivated by many Euro-Americans. The Caucasians who believe in and practice the humanity of all people and work to better the quality of life for all people in their sphere of influence are vastly outnumbered. To say the least, it is essential that parents obtain and discuss as much history of their family's mental-emotional health at it's 'source' to identify and treat maladies that are present in family matters.

Do you have any history of parents, grandparents or relatives using psychotropic medications; being institutionalized in a mental facility; learning disabilities, or deaths related to suicide? These are mental health concerns that your family must become aware of.

These experiences are just the tip of the mental-emotional iceberg submerged beneath the immediate view of most people until it surfaces in the individual, marital or family life. Returning to the source becomes part of the solution.

One more thought on mental-emotional healing: If some parents would just tell their child, "I'm sorry," that child could begin to heal and move on with his or her life. So many parents inhibit the health and healing of their child (many who are now adults) because they refuse to acknowledge personal offenses toward their children. Many are resentful and bitter to this very day because parents refuse to 'fess up' to the wrongs they have committed against them. You would be astonished to know how many people have never gotten over their parent's physical, mental and verbal abuse toward them. Some of them have a "love-hate" relationship with mama or daddy.

Some parents were so rigid and unyielding that they refused to give their child 'breathing room.' The child grew up naive and limited and he or she hasn't healed from it yet. I could go on and on, but you get the point. Many parents could free their children up with those two words, spoken in honesty and humility.

"I'm sorry," must be accompanied with an adequate and complete explanation of what you are sorry for and why. Rebekah never got a chance to tell her son Jacob that she was wrong or that she was sorry. She died before Jacob returned home.

Parents, don't go to the grave with your children resenting you the rest of their lives. You initiate the healing process in your family. If you have trouble expressing yourself, then get a qualified person to mediate. It's time to make that call or write that letter. You can finally be at peace.

Jacob wanted peace. His life was riddled with chaos and confusion. He longed to make things right with his brother and father. He determined to do just that the first chance he got, but he still had his fears. He didn't know that soon Jacob the conman would become the real fresh prince!

Statements of Reflection on Chapter 9:
1. If there is a primary goal all individuals, marriages and families need to accomplish it is healing. Healing cannot be accomplished without returning to the source.
2. Here's one of the biggest impediments to healing: Most grandparents and parents won't talk! They have key information that could unlock closets where family skeletons are hidden, but they won't say anything.
3. Inherited and cultivated traits that surface generation after generation could come to a screeching halt in many families if those who know the source would open up.
4. When families are hurting, true love does not keep silent.
5. We have to know the root to understand the fruit.
6. When a defect in character is identified and brought to our attention, it is a call to resolving or remedying it; a summons to mastery over it.
7. Family matters are surfacing earlier than ever before in children

and is having a more devastating effect on them than ever before.
8. If inherited traits are cultivated by the children, it may take them a lifetime to recover.
9. There are many children who have received a good, spiritual, principled upbringing with spiritual and principled parents, but do not know they have dormant inherited traits within. As long as they are not activated, they are not cultivated toward habits.
10. Children don't inherit spirituality from parents. Spirituality is not transferrable. Spirituality is a choice, not an endowment. That's something each person must choose for themselves.
11. We need to know the 'source' of all our family health problems; especially those that continue generationally. That not only includes physical health but also mental-emotional health.
12. No child should suffer because of our silence, embarrassing as it may be. Elders and parents must divulge all information that assists in the solution to family matters.
13. If some parents would just tell their children, "I'm sorry," that child could begin to heal.

THE REAL FRESH PRINCE 10

"The Angel of Yahweh said to me in a dream, 'Jacob,' and I answered, 'Here I am.' 'Arise and leave this land, and return to the land of your birth.' Then Jacob prepared and put his sons and wives on camels; and he took all his cattle and all the possessions he had acquired to take back to his father Isaac's home in Canaan. Laban had gone away to sheer sheep and Jacob did not tell Laban he was leaving, and he left with all his family and possessions without Laban knowing for three days. Laban gathered his men and chased after Jacob and caught them in the mountain at Gilead (Genesis 31:11, 13,17,18, 19-23)."

"And Jacob left that night and took his two wives, and his two maid servants, and his eleven children, and crossed over the Jabbok River with all his possessions. But he stayed on this side of the river alone. It was about midnight when a Man appeared out of nowhere as if to attack Jacob, and the two of them wrestled until just before daybreak. Now when the Stranger saw that Jacob would not release Him, He touched Jacob's hip and put it out of joint. (That's when Jacob knew he had been contending with Someone who had more than human power. So Jacob clung helplessly to the Man and asked for mercy.) The Man said, 'Let me go, it will soon be daybreak.' But Jacob said, 'I will not let you go until you bless me.' The Man said, "What is your name?" And he said, 'Jacob!' Then He said, "I'm changing your name. You'll no longer be called Jacob (which means 'heel grabber' or conman), but ISRAEL, (which means 'Prince of Yahweh Elohim) because you have wrestled with Me and you have won the blessing and assurance for which you have struggled" (Genesis 32:22-28).

After 21 bitter-sweet, guilt-ridden years, Jacob is on his way home to receive his inheritance. Haunted by painful memories, he knows it is time to buck up. The 'chicken' is coming home to roost! Chickens may stray from the farm, but before sunset, they always come back home.

To put it in contemporary terms: What goes around comes around, or, what goes down is coming up again! Everybody comes back down that same road sooner or later. Jacob had to face his past head-on if he was ever going to move forward. So must we. We must face our past if we expect to resolve it once and for all.

Going home is difficult for so many people. It was for Jacob. Unpleasant memories and experiences beg not to be exhumed. Dr. John Henrik Clarke said, "The past is always present." Past experiences affect our present reality. There is no escaping our past. The only solution is to face it and resolve it.

Jacob might have never gone back home if he had not been open to divine guidance. His upbringing was poor, his mistakes were great, and his fears were even greater. He feared facing his father Isaac who he had deceived and hurt deeply. He feared facing Esau his brother who had a contract out on his life. He feared fear itself.

Fear keeps many of you from returning to the source that can help you can move forward in your life. Fear of rejection, fear of failure; fear of intimacy, fear of sacrifice, fear of comment; fear of commitment and so on. These are destructive fears, not healthy fears, and do lead to all kinds of physical and mental health disorders that prolong family matters.

There is a healthy fear. We should fear rattlesnakes. The healthy fear of rattlesnakes leads to self preservation. If I see one, I'm running! But the other fears I just mentioned are unhealthy and do not lead to self or family preservation. They cause stress, cancer, paranoia, and other unnecessary maladies.

Unhealthy fear is really **false education accepted as reality**. Usually, these fears are greater than the actual situation. Have you ever experienced the fear of taking a test? Once the instructor handed you the test and you looked at it, you said, "This is easy." Your fear was greater than the actual situation. Your fear had blown it out of proportion. You were stressed out for nothing.

One scripture says, "For Yahweh did not give us a spirit of fear, but a spirit of love, power and a sound (adjusted) mind (2 Timothy 1:7)." Fear has decimated as many lives as war has. Fear hinders healing. We should no longer permit anything to impede our individual, marital or family healing.

Some challenges can be resolved with a book. Going to the library and getting a book on anger management and learning creative ways to resolve it may work for some of you. What some of us need is enlightenment from those who are not emotionally attached to our family matters to give us sound and objective ways of resolving anger. The key is to acknowledge our anger and identify the human or material resources to resolve it. That is one way of returning to move forward.

There are other family matters that are much more challenging and will take more time and effort to resolve, and like Jacob, you have to go 'home' to the source to begin the healing process.

It is important to communicate with your mother, father, or a knowledgeable relative, if your parents can't or won't communicate. Many of them hold the key that can open up a closet full of answers toward your solutions. It might not always be complete or adequate information but we can use what we can get to better understand the whole family portrait.

There comes a time in life (hopefully sooner than later) when we will have to face family matters. I can't say what will be the catalyst. Often its tragedy or crisis, but it doesn't have to be. Some parents are in denial until they have gotten to the point where they throw their hands up and say, "I don't know what to do with this child!" In their exasperation, they start making calls to try and find help. Now, they are open up to resolution. But by this time, that young person has had time to cultivate negative traits. But better late than never.

Laban is away sheering his sheep. Jacob gets the summons by Yahweh to return home. While Laban is gone, Jacob assembles his family, cattle and possessions together and sneak away. **We must recognize and utilize strategic and opportune times to resolve**

family matters. Many people have let family matters persist because they did not 'seize the moment' to initiate a resolution.

Jacob got a three-day jump on Laban before he got came home and found out Jacob had taken away his daughters, his servants and his grandchildren. When opportunities don't present themselves, we must make opportunities by making contact with someone who can assist us in our individual, marital or family healing.

I believe the healing process first begins with the one who admits he/she needs to be healed. But the healing process cannot be carried out by one's self. Healing is a collective dynamic of two or more participants. True and lasting healing requires an interdependency by consenting participants.

Jacob followed divine guidance and talked to his family. They responded in the affirmative and together, they cooperated in their solution. When Laban came home and discovered they were gone, he and his men chased after Jacob and his family.

More likely than not, you will encounter opposition as you seek healing. Don't expect everyone to cooperate wholeheartedly in your healing process. For instance, your parents may never open up and share critical information. I call it the "Laban Syndrome." Laban did not want to give in to Jacob and his family's restoration. He vehemently, even physically tried to deny the hope and healing they so desperately needed. Misery loves company. But if you have the will, there is a way.

The fascinating aspect of this episode is that Yahweh had already gone ahead of Jacob and taken care of the situation. Yahweh had spoken to Laban and told him he better not impede Jacob and his family from getting to their destination.

Laban played it off by saying that Jacob had left and had not given him a chance to kiss his daughters and grandchildren and say good bye (Genesis 31:22-54). Old, conniving, insecure Laban had sense enough to know his arms were too short to box with Yahweh!

When we want to be healed, opportunity is provided. Jacob wanted healing for his past, courage for his present and hope to his future. Yahweh provided the way and means to secure it.

I believe nobody can stop the Creator's plans for you but you! **There is no individual, marital or family matter that cannot be surmounted or resolved, even among opposition.**

Though Laban went back home, Esau was coming! One of Jacob's men was posted as a lookout. He informed Jacob that Esau was coming with 400 men who were armed. Jacob had to execute his family plan if they were to survive.

When you to read this encounter in Genesis chapter 33, you will see that Yahweh had spoken to Esau just has he had to Laban. Esau was warned not to harm Jacob. If you are willing to resolve your family matters, as the old African elders use to say, "God will make a way out of no way." But this way is one of active planning on our part, not some passive waiting for God to work a miracle.

Our own decisions are vital to our solutions and healing. The Creator provides us with a mind to plan and opportunities for resolution. We must make the plans and execute them. It is a cooperative effort. If we do nothing, nothing will get done. Faith without works is dead.

Twenty-one years of Jacob's life was dotted with unnecessary and unpleasant experiences all because he ripped off Esau. A large part of his life was lost because of denial, procrastination and fear. My point is, how much longer will you or your family go until you begin the healing process? Unless you make minor adjustments now concerning your past, you will reap even worse consequences in the future, especially your children! It is not necessary for them to have to struggle 21 years or more as adults (as some of us have done) with inherited and cultivated traits that we could and should be resolving now with a family plan. I quoted earlier: "It is easier to build a boy than it is to mend a man!" That goes for females also.

Yearly, I counsel so many adults who haven't known peace and contentment for the majority of their lives. Now they have children who are struggling with family matters, and it is not fair for parents or relatives to remain silent or apathetic when they can be part of their solution. It is unhealthy for any individual, marriage or family to put off the necessary planning and follow-through that will provide hope and healing.

To decide to get help, to return to the source to go forward, to plan and follow-through, to stop generational traits, are all conscious decisions. Not to make a decision is to make a decision. Since a decision must be made, it may as well be to go back and face the challenges and then move forward to healing. I know people who have done it. I am helping people to do it. It can be done. It must be done.

Too often, many try to live their lives without divine guidance. We cannot ignore the Creator and expect to live in harmony with humanity. My mother told me when I was a young, "If you're too busy for God, you're too busy." The time I had gotten "too busy for God," was the time I regret the most in my life. If some of you reflect back on your past, the regrets you have was when you (or your assailant) was too busy for God!

Just as a loving parent hurts for their wayward child, much more does the Creator hurt when we fail to follow the spiritual principles that are given for our health and well being.

Let me give an example that most of us have suffered the consequence for not following wholesome instruction. Most of us have had the flu. The physician prescribes an antibiotic. The instructions say to take one capsule three times a day for four days, drink plenty of liquids and rest in bed. On the second day, we start feeling better so we didn't take the antibiotic. Because we felt pretty good, we got up and jumped back into our daily routine (when the day before we were flat on our backs or in the bathroom!) That evening, we came home sick as a dog! You remember that? What happened? We didn't follow the instructions the physician gave!

There was a reason those specific instructions were given. The body needed rest, liquids and ALL of the antibiotics to fight off the flu. Now we felt worse than we did in the first place and we had to stay on our back longer than we would have if we had obeyed!

We have to do more than this resolved family matters. There are divine instructions and principles that we must follow if we are not to have a recurring bout with the same problems! Since we come from the Creator, who best knows how we may maintain harmony in our lives, marriages, families and society than the Creator? Unless we study and inculcate the Creator's divine and natural principles in our individual, marital or family lives, relapse will take place and it may be worse than the first time!

The Creator's spiritual principles rest on the foundation of Love. If humanity practiced love, no child would ever be raped, murdered and eaten by a human being! No spouse would ever feel a dagger in their heart by a spouse who committed adultery! The deadly military industrial complex would "beat their swords into plows and their spears into pruning hooks," and study war no more! Prisons and psyche wards would virtually be empty! And individuals, marriages and families would be restored if humanity lived by the Creator's divine and natural principles.

I am not trying to sound idealistic; I'm being realistic. The human family is reaping what it has sown! The sadistic statistics of the inhumanity of man-against-man means we are reaping the inevitable consequences of violating the divine and natural principles of the Creator. If the statement, "as goes the family, so goes society," is true, then spirituality must be at the center of the family if it is to permeate society.

I am not talking about religion. Religion is based on preference and affiliation. I'm referring to spirituality, which is based on relationship, which practices a love for the Creator and a principled respect for human and natural creation. The plan of each family should be: Spirituality, Health and Prosperity! In that order, hope and healing will be restored to our families.

Wrestling

Jacob had one final encounter before he returned to the source in order to go forward. I call it Wrestling. Jacob was so close to being restored, but he jeopardized his healing and restoration by wrestling.

Don't miss my point: The very opportunity we need to take advantage of, often, we fight against it. Many of you wrestle against the very thing you need: Healing. Why keep wrestling? All you're doing is putting your future in peril.

I have seen people who have suffered and want relief, but don't want to change their lifestyle. Many diseases are prevalent with certain lifestyles, but some people only want to eliminate the disease but not the lifestyle that attracts the disease, so they wrestle.

There are husbands and wives who know their marriage is on the rocks. Most of the family matters they experience comes from inherited or cultivated traits that could be identified and resolved. With positive intervention, their marriage could become all that it should be. But one spouse wrestles and refuses to go to counseling. These are just a couple of the many sad scenarios where people could be healed but refuse.

Wrestling is a mindset where we refuse to relinquish our grip, our position, our defensiveness, our opinion, our hurts, our lifestyle, etc., and we worsen our family matters.

Our family matters should not go from bad to worse, but they do when we wrestle. When we recognize unresolved inherited or cultivated traits but refuse any plan of healing, that's wrestling. Wrestling can worsen physical and mental-emotional health or strain marital and family relations.

Jacob's wrestling affected his physical health. Jacob limped the rest of his life. When we wrestle against the principles of health, we may not be restored in our physical health the rest of our lives! When you go back and discover that high blood pressure has generationally affected your family, it is wise to do what is necessary to prevent it by eliminating the foods or factors that perpetuate it. Cut the salt. Get off meat, especially pork. Drink more water. Exercise daily. Stop living to eat and eat to live. Simplify your lifestyle and reduce stress. Do what it takes to prevent high blood pressure from antagonizing you and your children.

Whatever physical or mental health-related condition has

plagued your family, stop wrestling and start making the decisions that will add longevity and stability to your life and your family's.

Whatever areas of immorality, temperament, or behavior you have recognized as generational in your family, they will never be eliminated while you are wrestling. Jacob came to the realization that it was futile to wrestle. Wrestling gets tiring after while. The three primary reasons why so many of us continue to wrestle is denial, procrastination and fear. All three impede our healing.

Denial

Denial is wrestling. Denial is tiring. Continual denial becomes a habit as strong as any physical addiction. Denial is a mental-emotional addiction rooted in faulty thinking. Denial tries to convince us that things are not as bad as we think. Denial conceals pertinent information that could assist in healing. Family matters persist for years because denial holds hope and healing hostage.

The first step in being rid of denial is to acknowledge denial for what it really is. Denial is deadly. Denial has no redeeming virtues, nor can its nature change. It is what it is: the enemy of hope and healing.

Secondly, denial is like harboring a deadly enemy. We must deny harboring denial in our lives, marriages and families. Denial will attack any positive change we plan in our lives. Denial is detrimental to us, and destroys the hope and healing we so desperately need, while we give it sanctuary or refuge.

Lastly, denial is a decision. Since denial is a decision, denial can be denied control of our lives. Some might think it's easier to keep skeletons in the family closet or forego returning to the source in order to move forward with our lives. But they have no peace, and those skeletons rattle something terrible!

Honesty ousts denial. Honesty denies refuge to denial. Until we can be honest with ourselves and others, hope and healing will never be accomplished. Denial incarcerates, but honesty liberates. Don't you long to be free from the family matters that bind you?

No relationship can grow without honesty. That includes a relationship with yourself. Before you can have a wholesome relationship with others, you must have one with yourself. If you will not be honest with yourself, you cannot be honest with anyone else. Honesty begins with you. Evict denial with honesty.

Procrastination
Procrastination is wrestling. Procrastination is tiring. Procrastination offers false hope. Procrastination is like a striptease. It tantalizes and arouses but never satisfies or fulfills its promises. The promise of taking care of the problem (sooner or later) remains just out of reach. How many more years will you wrestle when solutions are only a decision away? How many more of our children will be caught in the middle of nasty divorces because the unrecognized or unresolved traits of surfaced in their marriage and resolving them was put off time and time again?

It didn't have to take Jacob 21 years to go back to the source to go forward. Procrastination was a big part of his problem. It is not fair to yourself, your marriage or family for you to put off any longer the family matters you recognize as detrimental in your home. Jacob extended his family matters longer than he should have. The very nature of procrastination keep us wrestling with the same family matters day-in and day-out, generation after generation.

There are realities in life that cannot afford to be put off. Procrastinate on your mortgage or rent and foreclosure or eviction is inevitable. Procrastinate on putting gas in your car and you'll get stuck on the side of the road somewhere disgusted with yourself. Procrastinate on your physical or mental well-being and hospitalization is the result. So why procrastinate on family matters?

Procrastination is a decision. Since we make decisions daily, just as we decided to procrastinate, we can decide to prioritize. Organization is the conqueror of procrastination. This is where a 'things to do list' in an organizer becomes vital to planning and follow-through. Commit to purchasing an organizer and list according to priority, the things you need to do to access family healing.

Share this idea of organization with family members and close friends so they can motivate and encourage you to follow-through with your plans. Refer to your organizer as much as you need to. List names, numbers and appointments for individual, marital or family counseling, etc. Getting organized is the antidote for procrastination. It will also enhance other areas of your life.

Fear

Fear is wrestling. Fear is tiring too. Fear may be the biggest impediment to healing. So many people have a fear of rejection, fear of failure, fear of intimacy, fear of the truth, etc. Fear is an emotion fueled by a desire to avoid pain or keep from being harmed; yet fear has done more to immobilize hope and healing than any other enemy except death.

So many people embrace fear, not recognizing that fear is our enemy. Fear is against us, not for us. By harboring fear, we are harboring the archenemy of hope and healing. Think about it. We are harboring, feeding and housing our enemy.

Let's give Jacob some credit. Though he had some fears, he did not let them paralyze him in inaction. Once Jacob overcame the first two roadblocks to healing, denial and procrastination, he could confront his fears. He could have died at Laban's place and could have never had the chance to salvaged the rest of his life. But you can salvage your life, marriage, and your family!

If Jacob never left Laban's place, his children would have remained in a strange land, incarcerated by their father's denial, procrastination and fears. If we let fear paralyze us, our children will be incarcerated by our negative inherited and cultivated traits that arrested positive character development.

Fear is a decision. It takes something stronger than fear to be liberated from it. The scripture says, "There is no fear in love. Love casts out fear, because fear causes torment. The one who fears does not grow in love" (1 John 4:18). Love is the greatest liberator from fear.

Love for your family can break the grip of fear and stop generational family matters. Your healing process becomes love in action! The O'Jays of Cleveland, Ohio sang a song called Love Train. "Get on board the Love Train...if you miss it, I feel sorry for you."

Denial, procrastination and fear are like a tag team in a wrestling ring. After we have had a long grueling bout with denial, we say we are going to do something about our family matters. But denial tags procrastination who grabs us before we get out the ring. Procrastination takes over and throws us for a loop. Only when we are hurt bad enough (physically/emotionally) do we say that we are going to get help. But procrastination senses we are finally serious and tags fear. Fear is the biggest of the three. Fear throws all kinds of questions at us to wrestle with. What if your spouse doesn't want to go to counseling? What will your children think of you when they find out your past? Will you ever be able to trust your child again?

Fear has the tightest grip of the tag team. Fear is the 'Hulk Hogan' that is reeking havoc in our family matters. Mba Mbulu said, "Fear is one of the most natural emotions. Therefore, no one can be blamed or ridiculed for responding to a threatening situation in a fearful manner. However, there are times when it is necessary to control your response to fear; to analyze what is causing the fear and determine if the risk to your health or security (or whatever) is worth enduring."

Wrestling is tiring. Wrestling resolves nothing. Wrestling is a decision. Jacob stopped wrestling and started holding on. Holding on to what? That which was within his reach; that which was within his ability to change.

Individuals and families must grab hold of the human and material resources that will assist in resolving family matters. It is at this juncture that follow-through is crucial.

I'll use myself as an example again. One of my family challenges was the lack of adequate finances. Though my wife and I work, we still have to 'pinch pennies.' We do not squander our money. We stick to our budget. One alternative was to cut our expenses. After taking a financial assessment, We consolidated our small debts with a loan and paid them off. Instead of five monthly payments, we only have one.

We also identified where we could cut interest costs and fees for service by changing banks and refinancing our car through a credit union. We don't buy on credit anymore. We are saving by reducing debt and finding lower interest rates. Now we are exploring creative ways to increase our income.

There are so many resources that are out there and available to resolve **all** family matters. But nobody's going to read your mind, call you on the telephone, or ask you do you need their assistance. Yahshua the Messiah said, "Ask and it shall be given; seek and you will find; knock and it will be opened to you (Matthew 7:7)." This must be your initiative. This is your impetus to hope and healing.

Once we stop wrestling with denial, procrastination and fear, we are half-way to the answers we need. Planning and patience is the other half. Miracles do happen but all of them do not come overnight. Our consolation is that we are actively doing something to resolve our family matters by finding and utilizing human and material resources.

When Yahweh said to Jacob, "Let me go," Jacob replied, "Not until you bless (help) me." When you have the will, there is a way. When you have the desire, you do not accept defeat. You hold on until your hope and healing comes! Some goals take a little longer than others. But when it comes to family matters: WE HAVE NOTHING TO LOSE BUT OUR CHAINS!

What Is Your Name?

"And He said, "What is your name?" And he said, 'Jacob.' Your name will no longer be called Jacob, but Israel; for you have wrestled with Yahweh and have prevailed" (Genesis 32:27-28). The name "Israel" means, "Prince of Elohim" (God). Jacob became "the real fresh prince!" He is putting a 'period' behind his past and writing a new chapter for his future.

Deeper still, the old names (labels) that dogged his steps, like 'heel grabber,' 'conman,' 'deceiver,' and the like, are now behind him. By changing his name, Yahweh closed the door to Jacob's past and opened one to his future.

If you want to know who you really are, your true identity does not lie in what you have done or what has happened to you in the past. Your true identity lies in what you have committed yourself to becoming!

What is your name? What you think of yourself will be how you name (label) yourself. Is it a positive name? Does it express hope of your future? Is it really possible to go from a conman to a prince? Is it possible to acquire a healthy attitude of your future with such a painful past? Only if you think so.

"Two men where in prison, both looked through the bars; one looked at the mud, the other at the stars." What made the difference? How you look at your situation. Regardless of your family matters, you are still free to choose your attitude in any situation. Someone rightly said: "If you can conceive it, and believe it, you can achieve it." You must replace negative thinking with positive thinking. You must conceive your goal before you can achieve your goal.

The African proverb says, "Once you have received a vision, it cannot be returned." Yahweh was giving Jacob a vision of what he could and would become, even before he returned to the source to go forward with his life.

You will rise no higher than the level of your thinking. And there are times when we must permit someone else to elevate our thought processes. Positive affirmation goes a long way in lifting our spirits. But nothing will usurp how you think about yourself. You have the final say-so.

Jacob could have rejected a new mindset ("prince") and stubbornly kept the name "Jacob." Consequently, he would have risen no higher than what he thought about himself. But "Israel" had a goal in mind, and he would use any positive means necessary to reach his goal.

Whatever is positive and principled that is part of our solution, we must use it for our healing. It may be as simple as someone affirming us, to following-up a helpful suggestion or a time-honored commitment to complete counseling/therapy. **What is your name?**

Statements of Reflection on Chapter 10:
1. Everybody comes back down that same road sooner or later.
2. Past experiences affect our present reality. There is no escaping our past. The only solution is to face it and resolve it .
3. Fear keeps many of you from returning to the source so you can move forward in your life.
4. Unhealthy fear is really false education accepted as reality.
5. Some of us need is enlightenment from those who are not emotionally attached to our family matters to give us sound and objective ways of resolving anger.
6. We must recognize and utilize strategic and opportune times to resolve family matters. Many people have let family matters persist because they did not 'seize the moment' to initiate a resolution.
7. I believe the healing process first begins with the one admits he/she needs to be healed. But the healing process cannot be carried out by one's self. Healing is a collective dynamic of two or more participants. True and lasting healing requires an interdependency by consenting participants.
8. There is no individual, marital or family matter that cannot be surmounted or resolved, even among opposition.
9. The Creator provides us with a mind to plan and opportunities for resolution. We must make the plans and execute them. It is a cooperative effort. If we do nothing, nothing will get done. Faith without works is dead.
10. To decide to get help; to return to the source to go forward; to plan and follow-through; to stop generational traits, is conscious decision.
11. The plan of each family should be: Spirituality, Health and Prosperity! In that order, hope and healing will be restored to our

families.

12. Wrestling is a mindset where we refuse to relinquish our grip, our position, our defensiveness, our opinion, our hurts, our lifestyle, etc., and we worsen our family matters.

13. Whatever physical or mental health-related condition has plagued your family, stop wrestling and start making the decisions that will add longevity and stability to your life and your family's.

14. The three primary reasons why so many of us continue to Wrestle is denial, procrastination and fear. They worsen our family matters and impede our healing.

15. Family matters persist for years because denial holds hope and healing hostage.

16. Honesty ousts denial. Honesty denies refuge to denial. Until we can be honest with ourselves and others, hope and healing will never be accomplished.

17. Procrastination keep us wrestling with the same family matters day-in and day-out; generation after generation.

18. Love for your family can break the grip of fear and stop generational family matters. Your healing process becomes love in action!

MINOR ADJUSTMENTS
11

"And Yahweh said to Jacob, 'Go to Beth-el, and reside there. Build an altar to Yahweh who appeared to you there when you ran from Esau your brother.' Jacob said to his family and to all who were with him, 'Put away your strange gods, bathe yourselves and change your clothes. We must leave and go to Beth-el where I will build an altar unto Yahweh, who answered me in the day of my trouble, and has never left me, no matter where I have gone' (Genesis 35:1-3)."

After more than twenty years, Jacob faced his 'family matters.' He stopped wrestling with denial, procrastination and fear, and executed a plan of action. Notice what Jacob instructs his family to do: a) Put away strange gods b) Wash and put on clean clothes c) Go to Beth-el and build an altar unto Yahweh. This is how I interpret Jacob's instructions: There are things that are necessary for us to put out of our lives and things that are essential to add to our lives. Our families must make some minor adjustments if we are to be healed.

I read an article by James LeNoir entitled, Dialectics of Success. This article explained how to reach goals or seek solutions to problems. Dialectics is defined as "systematic reasoning, exposition, or argument that juxtaposes opposed or contradictory ideas that seeks to resolve their conflict." Mr. LeNoir teaches, "All life and nature are dialectical. This means that everything results from the interaction of at least two things. Nothing is the cause of itself; and nothing has just one cause."

In resolving family matters, we cannot accomplish it by ourselves. There must be the interaction of at least two 'key' components (that are usually opposites) when seeking a solution. Here are three tips that LeNoir suggests for bringing about change in your life and for achieving goals:

All change is produced either by addition or subtraction. We must either add to or subtract from the existing situation.

For example, your associates. Either you need to add positive associates who can assist you in accomplishing your goals, or you must subtract those associates who are an impediment to your progress and healing?

If the cause of your problem is "A" then you must add the opposite of "A." If your problem is procrastination, then you must add the opposite of procrastination, which is actively initiating an organized plan of action to resolve that problem.

Discipline bridges the gap between knowing what needs to be done and actually doing it. Most of us know 'what' we need to do to be healed, but lack the will power to do what needs to be done. When we discipline ourselves to do something specific each day, that is part of our solution, our healing; it may be resolved sooner than we think.

This is just the skeleton. You must put the flesh on the bones of each point. You must decide what you must add or subtract to reach your goals. You must decide what 'opposite' to add to the cause of your problems. Finally, you must discipline yourself to do some solution-oriented activity each day for your healing.

Progress is made one step at a time. Too many of us get overwhelmed because we see a gigantic problem looming so large, we feel we can't make a dent in it. If it has been going on for years, the likelihood of resolving it becomes improbable. Denial, procrastination and fear become the inevitable result.

Jacob made the necessary minor adjustments. He instructed his family to subtract 'strange gods' from their lives. They put away everything that impeded their complete recovery. Next, they added those necessities that would assist their physical and mental-emotional health. Finally, they recovered their family spiritual health and well-being.

The blessing in our hope and healing is that we don't have to go it alone. We can't. Just as different parts of the body must interact to effect healing, as humans and families, we must cooperate to realize healing. It starts with minor adjustments.

"When Jacob left Mesopotamia, Yahweh visited him again and blessed him. Yahweh said to him, 'Your name is Jacob. But you will not be called Jacob any longer. You will be called Israel.' Yahweh said to him, 'I am the Almighty. Be fruitful and multiply. You will be the ancestor of nations and kings. The same land I gave to Abraham and Isaac, I will give to you and your descendants.' (Genesis 35:9-13)."

Yahweh talked to Jacob a second time. Yahweh asked Jacob again, "What is your name?" Then Yahweh reiterated to him his new name. "You will be called Israel." Yahweh's second naming ceremony for the man formally know as Jacob, may seem like a minor adjustment, but is has major implications. Something as minor as changing a name (label) can change a person's present and future outlook on life.

Too many of you are limited by the names (labels) you have accepted. For example, the so-called 'class system' in America relegates people to a distinct segment in society. These designations are based on socioeconomic stratification.

A family may be 'poor' as a result of the lack of economic or material resources but that same family may be 'rich' in love, optimism and positive community involvement. Are they poor or rich? It depends on what name (label) they accept for themselves.

Many families are labeled 'dysfunctional.' This name is usually attached to one-parent families. But is 'dysfunctional' a state of being or a state of mind? The majority of those parenting alone are not 'dysfunctional,' but 'mo-functional!' They have to use 'mo-creativity,' 'mo-ingenuity,' 'mo-with-less,' to keep their children clothed and fed! When it comes to names (labels), you are not what you think you are, but what you think, you are.

Some of you have a painful past of verbal abuse. You were

called some ugly names! But when you minor adjustments in your thinking, you are liberated from those labels. (Someone rightly said, "It's not what you call me but what I answer to.") This is not a denial of your past, but it is an optimistic view for your future.

When you look back over the family of Abraham, Isaac and Jacob, you will see that Yahweh is in the business of changing names. Abram to Abraham, Sarai to Sarah, and Jacob to Israel. Why? Because Family Matters!

Yahweh changed Abram's name to Abraham. Abraham means "father of a multitude." Though Abraham started out with a small family, Yahweh's vision was for his progeny to grow and prosper.

Sarah was so preoccupied with the pain of not having a child that Yahweh needed her to focus on the potential of her future. Yahweh changed her name to Sarah which means "princess."

The Creator has the most healthy view of us when we don't have one of ourselves. When we are focusing on impossibilities, the Creator is focusing on our possibilities. The Creator thinks the best of us when we think the worst of ourselves.

When we have consigned ourselves with being "Jacob," the rest of our lives, the Creator has already envisioned for us a new name and a new start. When people putt us down, the Creator wants to lift us up! When 'family matters' of a painful past looms large in our lives, the Creator is looking at the finished product; that is, a life, a marriage, a family restored to wholeness.

It all begins with minor adjustments. Minor adjustments begin in our thought processes. Major changes in life come from minor adjustments. **Minor adjustments are a series of steps that will add to the solution while subtracting from the problem.** Discouragement usually sets in when we try to solve the whole problem in one session. It takes time and patience to work through 'family matters.' Anything of quality is usually not accomplished overnight. Your hope lies in the fact that you have planned your work (healing process) and you are working your plan. Minor adjustments are step-by-step decisions that lead to eventual resolution of family matters.

As necessary as healing was for Jacob, healing was not his final objective. Jacob's ultimate aim was RECONCILIATION. Jacob didn't just want to get right, he wanted to get it right with his family (Esau and his father Isaac). **Reconciliation must be the goal of all our individual, marital and family relationships.** Reconciliation is the act of restoring harmony or friendship. Can you imagine how exciting it would be to have strained and broken relationships reconciled?

Although we cannot guarantee the response of family members, (or acquaintances) we can at least initiate reconciliation on our part. If we wait for them to make the first move, it may never happen. At least we can be at peace for attempting to make amends, as well as remain open to reconcile should we have opportunity at a later time. Again, we have nothing to lose but our chains!

If we are not able to reconcile with a family member, (as in the case of Jacob whose mother had died before he returned home); if we are healed to the point that we would if we had the opportunity, then our willingness to reconcile is accepted by the Creator as if we carried out the act of reconciliation. If we refuse to reconcile, that is an indication of an unforgiving heart. We are not truly healed unless we truly forgive.

True reconciliation can never take place without forgiveness. When we are willing to forgive those who have wronged us, and willing to receive forgiveness from those we have wronged, reconciliation is possible.

Jacob finally secured hope, healing, and reconciliation. **It's not where we start out, but where we end up that proves beyond a doubt, that "Family Matters!"**

Statements of Reflection on Chapter 11:
1. There are things that are necessary for us to put out of our lives and things that are essential to add to our lives.
2. In resolving family matters, we cannot accomplish it by ourselves. There must be the interaction of at least two 'key' components.

3. All change is produced either by addition or subtraction. We must either add to or subtract from the existing situation.
4. Discipline bridges the gap between knowing what needs to be done and actually doing it.
5. The Creator has the most healthy view of us when we don't have one of ourselves. When we are focusing on impossibilities, the Creator is focusing on our possibilities. The Creator thinks the best of us when we think the worst of ourselves.
6. Something as minor changing a name (label) can change a person's present and future outlook on life. Too many individuals and families are limited by the names (labels) they have accepted.
7. Minor adjustments are a series of steps that will add to the solution while subtracting from the problem.
8. Reconciliation must be the goal of all our individual, marital and family relationships. Reconciliation is the act of restoring harmony or friendship.
9. True reconciliation can never take place without forgiveness. When we are willing to forgive and willing to receive forgiveness from those we have wronged, reconciliation is possible.
10. If we refuse to reconcile, that is an indication of an unforgiving heart. We are not truly healed unless we truly forgive.
11. It's not where we start out, but where we end up that proves beyond a doubt, that "Family Matters!"

APPENDIX

- Begin Your Healing Process
- Family Matters Questionnaire
- Marriage Questionnaire
- Individual Questionnaire
- Family Matters Inventory
- Resolving Conflicts In Families
- Identifying Resources For Healing
- 1-800 Resource Listing, Etc.
- Self-Help Reading List for General Population
- Self-Help Reading List for African Americans
- Selected Bibliography

BEGIN YOUR HEALING PROCESS

This appendix is simply a 'starter' to help you begin your healing process. The three areas that are addressed are: Individual, Marriage and Family. The objective is to help you:

1. Identify the areas of your individual life where personal healing is needed.

2. Identify marital challenges that need to be resolved.

3. Identify family matters that need to be addressed, resolved and/or mediated.

4. Identify and contact resources needed for healing and/or resolution. (Resources include parents, relatives, qualified persons, support groups, etc.).

5. Identify and read self-help books that offer hope and healing.

Family Matters Questionnaire

All family matters must be worked through and worked out. There are no short cuts in complete healing. There are three steps in the healing process: First, a family profile (history) must be done. Next, an examination (diagnosis) of the problem. Finally, a plan of healing (recovery).

The purpose of this questionnaire is to help you return to the source to move forward. Some of your parents/grandparents are deceased or will not talk. You need a structured way of returning to the source (if possible) to identify specific aspects of your upbringing in order to give you a point of reference in your healing process.

Answer each question with a complete and thorough answer. Although you may not complete the questionnaire at one sitting, work on it a little each day. It won't take long to complete. Write your answers in a composition book instead of on loose leaf paper so that you can keep them together. When you finish, you will have chronicled a fairly extensive review of your upbringing.

I suggest you complete this questionnaire before you talk with your parents, grandparents, relatives, etc. Your thoughts will be more organized and focused. Remember, this exercise is not about blaming- it's about healing. Don't procrastinate.

1. Describe each immediate family member. Immediate family includes parents and siblings. Description should focus on personality characteristics.

2. Describe the environment you grew up in. Describe the neighborhood, family, house, school and church (extended family and close relatives, if applicable).

3. Where there any special family traditions that were followed? Give examples.

4. Discuss how family members were treated? Was there a 'favorite' child? A 'trouble' child? Give examples.

5. How was family conflict handled? For example, when a problem arose was blame, criticism, or silence used? Give examples.

6. How did family members express anger? Give examples.

7. What issues were taboo or unacceptable topics that could not be discussed?

8. Was education considered important in your family? Give examples.

9. What family member has had the greatest influence upon your life? (Such as mother, father, siblings, grandparents, etc.) Please describe their influence upon your life.

10. What did they do to influence your life? Did they set good examples, talk to you, beat you, abuse you, etc.) Give examples.

11. Was their influence good or bad? Are you a better person or a bitter person?

12. What person outside your family had the greatest influence on you? (Such as a best friend, t.v. star, a drug pusher, an athlete, etc. How did they influence you?

13. Would you rear your children the same way your parents reared you? Why or why not? What would you do differently?

14. Did your parents build up your self-confidence or destroy it? How and why did they do this? [14]

FAMILY MATTERS INVENTORY

Identify and underline areas of your life, marriage and family that pertain to you. These are the areas that need to be resolved.

Alcoholism Anger Anorexia Bitterness Bolemia
Divorce Discord Depression Drug Use Disorganization
Family Problems Forgetfulness Forcefulness Guilt Hatred
Health Problems Hardheaded Insecure Insensitive Liar
Marriage Problems Procrastination Rape Victim Resentment
Suicidal Thoughts Stress Unwed Pregnancy Unforgiving
Unemployment Violent

Abuse: Physical Mental-Emotional Sexual Verbal

Finances: Disorganized Poor Management Skills Debt Problem Budgeting

Fear of: Failure Intimacy Love Rejection Authority

Lack of: Identity Education Motivation Self-Confidence Direction Meaning in Life

Self: Abuse Anger Hate Rejection Centered

Separation from: Family Spouse Children

Others:
1.
2.
3.

Marriage Questionnaire

1. List three positives in your marriage.
Wife:
a.
b.
c.
Husband:
a.
b.
c.

2. List three negatives in your marriage.
Wife:
a.
b.
c.
Husband:
a.
b.
c.

3. What would you rate as your number one marital challenge?
Wife:
a.
Husband:
a.

4. What (if any) are the 'outside' influences that positively affect your marriage?
Wife:
a.
b.

c.
Husband:
a.
b.
c.

5. What (if any) are the 'outside' influences that negatively affect your marriage?
Wife:
a.
b.
c.
Husband:
a.
b.
c.

6. What will **you** commit to do to resolve your marital challenges?
Wife:
a.
b.
c.

Husband:
a.
b.
c.

INDIVIDUAL QUESTIONNAIRE

Answer each question with <u>complete</u> answers.

1. What three positive (primary) traits do you think you have inherited from your parents?
a.
b.
c.

2. What three negative (primary) traits do you think you have inherited from your parents?
a.
b.
c.

3. What traits (inherited or cultivated) still need to be eliminated or resolved?
a.
b.
c.
d.
e.

4. List in order of priority the traits needing to be resolved.
a.
b.
c.
d.
e.

5. Write a 'mission statement' (paragraph) you will commit yourself to follow through to:

a. Maximize the positive traits you listed.

b. Resolve the negative traits you prioritized.

Resolving Conflicts In Families

1. **Establish Ground Rules** (List the rules. The less, the better).
a. One person speaks at a time. No interruptions.
b.
c.
d.
e.

2. **Outline The Problem(s)** (Don't try to discuss them all at one sitting. Plan resolution sessions.)

3. **Discuss One Problem At A Time**
a. Allow each participant time to discuss problems and feelings.
b. Identify and list each participant's concerns.

4. **List Several Solutions**
a. Solicit and write ideas for solutions from each participant.

5. **Evaluate The Solutions Together**

7. **Choose Solutions That Please All Participants.**
a. Be specific (when, where, how, how much, etc.)

8. **Come Together and Evaluate Solutions Periodically**

9. **Use A Trained Mediator If Needed.**
a. Ask a person (non-family member) trained in conflict resolution to mediate family sessions.

Identifying Resources for Healing

What is a resource system?
In simple terms it is a system which provides people with the necessary resources to address and resolve their needs and problems. In almost all communities, three kinds of resources are available: Informal, formal or membership, and societal. Informal resources consist of family, friends and co-workers. Formal resources consist of membership organizations or formal associations that exist to promote the mutual benefits and common interests of its members. The third resource exists through social legislation and voluntary citizen action to deliver services. (Hospitals, schools, daycare, etc.)

How can you find out about the resources in your community?
a. Consult your neighborhood or city directories for agencies that address your specific needs.

b. Develop your own community resource data listing. It should list special functions, kinds of services offered, and to whom they are offered.

c. Your resource data listing should also include: Name of resource, addresses, phone numbers, contact persons, time services are provided, and eligibility requirements.

1-800 RESOURCE LISTING, ETC.

24-Hour AIDS Hotline   800-342-AIDS
24 Hour Child Abuse Hotline   800-422-4453
24-Hour Cocaine Hotline   800-COCAINE
24-Hour Domestic Violence Hotline   800-333-7233
24-Hour Missing Children Hotline 800-843-5678 /782-7335
AL-NON (Support for alcohol recovery)   800-344-2666
ALATEEN (Support for teens)   800-356-999
National Clearinghouse Drugs/Alcohol Info 800-662-HELP
Runaway Hotline   800-621-4000
Prostitution and Pornography   800-551-1300
Sexually Transmitted Disease Hotline   800-227-8922
Hit-Home, National Youth Crisis Hotline   800-448-4663
Victims of Child Abuse Laws (falsely accused) 800-745-8778
Organ Donors   800-528-2971
Parents Without Partners   800-637-7974
Family Anonymous   800-736-9805
Kids Peace   800-858-KIDS

Additional Resources: (Regular Listings/ Addresses)
Prepare Our Youth, Inc.   (202) 291-5040
Self-Help Clearinghouse   (703) 941-5465
Children's Defense Fund 25 E. St. Washington, DC 20001
Mothers of Murdered Offspring (M.O.M.-O)(704) 372-7331
Maximum Life Enhancement   (205) 461-1019
Concerned Black Students   (205) 533-2012

For a comprehensive national resource book, contact:
Help For Children From Infancy to Adulthood
Rocky River Publishers P.O. Box 1679
Shepherdstown, WV 25443   800-343-068

SELF-HELP SUGGESTED READING LIST - GENERAL READING

Physical
God's Way To Health - George Malkmus
May All Be Fed: Diet For A New World - John Robbins

Mental-Emotional
Think Big - Dr. Ben Carson
Never Good Enough: Breaking Dependency - Carol Cannon

Spiritual
Hinds Feet In High Places - Hannah Hurnard

Social
Two Nations: Separate and Unequal - Andrew Hacker
The Measure of Our Success - Miriam Wright Edelman
Race: What Blacks and Whites Think - Studs Terkel
For Whites Only - Robert Terry

Relational
When Opposites Attract - Rebecca Cutter
Back To Basics - Arlene Taylor

Economic
Making Ends Meet - Henry E. Felder
Complete Financial Guide For Single Parents - L. Burkett

Education
The Myth Of The Hyperactive Child - P. Schrag/D. Divoky
Savage Inequalities - Jonathan Kozol

SELF-HELP SUGGESTED READING LIST FOR AFRICAN AMERICANS

Physical
African Wholistic Health - Llaila Afrika
The Black Women's Health Book - Evelyn Smith
They Stole It, But You Must Return It - Richard Williams
Good Health For African Americans - B. Dixon/J. Wilson

Mental-Emotional
The Miseducation of the Negro - Carter G. Woodson
Chains & Images of Psychological Slavery - Na'im Akbar
The Psychopathic Racial Personality - Bobby Wright

Spiritual
What Makes Great Great - Dennis Kimbro
Just A Sister Away - Renita Weems
Black Presence In The Bible - Walter McCray
Woman, Thou Art Loosed - T.D. Jakes
Why Most Black Men Don't Go To Church - Jawanza Kunjufu

Social
The Rage of A Privileged Class - Ellis Cose
The Endangered Black Family - Nathan & Julia Hare
Black Men: Single, Dangerous, Obsolete - Haki Madhubuti
Don't Believe The Hype - Farai Chideya
The Isis Papers - Francis Cress Welsing

(Relational)
Rearing African Children - Kwame Ronnie Vanderhorst
The Best Kind Of Loving - Gwendolyn Goldsby Grant
Counseling African American Couples - Clarence Walker

Cultural
Afrocentricity - Molefi K. Asante
Kwanzaa - Maulana Karenga
Coming of Age: Male Rites of Passage - Paul Hill
Transformation: Female Rites of Passage - Warfield
Nile Valley Contributions: Exploding The Myths - Anthony Browder

SELF-HELP SUGGESTED READING LIST - FOR AFRICAN AMERICANS (Con't)

Economics
Success Runs In Our Race - George Fraser
Work, Sister, Work - Cydney Shields/Leslie C. Shields
Black Labor, White Wealth - Dr. Claud Anderson
Think and Grow Rich - Dennis Kimbro
Money Issues in Black Male/Female Relationships -George Surbia

Education
Educating African Children - Kwame Ronnie Vanderhorst
The Maroon Within Us - Asa G. Hilliard
Introduction to Black Studies - Maulana Karenga
100 Best Colleges For African Americans - Erlene Wilson
Black Children: Roots, Culture & Learning - J. Hale-Benson
Countering the Conspiracy To Destroy Black Boys- Jawanza Kunjufu

SELECTED BIBLIOGRAPHY

1. Cain Hope Felder, Original African Heritage Study Bible (Nashville: James C. Winston Publishing Company, 1993)
2. Walter A. McCray, The Black Presence In The Bible (Chicago: Black Light Fellowship, 1990)
3. Anthony Browder, Nile Valley Contributions To Civilization (Washington, D.C.: Institute of Karmic Guidance, 1995)
4. John L. Johnson, The Black Biblical Heritage (St. Louis: The Black Biblical Heritage Publishing Company, 1975)
5. Max I. Dimont, Jews, God and History (New York: Simon and Shuster, 1962)
6. The Interpreter's Dictionary of the Bible (Nashville: Abingdon Press, 1962)
7. Johann Blumenbach, Encyclopedia Americana, (Vol. 4, 1994)
8. Watchman Nee, Spiritual Reality or Obsession (New York: Christian Fellowship Publishers, Inc. 1979)
9. E. White, Mind, Character & Personality (Nashville: Southern Publishing Association, 1977).
10. Charles Hummel, Tyranny of the Urgent (Illinois: Inter-Varsity Press, 1994)
11. Dr. Na'im Akbar, Chains and Images of Psychological Slavery (Jersey City: New Mind Productions, 1987)
12. Dr. Claud Anderson, Black Labor, White Wealth (Edgewood: Duncan & Duncan, Inc., Publishers
13. Cedric X (Clarke), D. Phillip McGee, Wade Nobles and Na'im Akbar, Voodoo Or IQ: An Introduction to African Psychology (Chicago:Institute of Positive Education, 1976)
14. Atieno Rosemary Scott (Clinical Psychologist)

AVAILABLE NOW!

REARING AFRICAN CHILDREN UNDER AMERICAN OCCUPATION
KWAME RONNIE VANDERHORST

"REARING AFRICAN CHILDREN UNDER AMERICAN OCCUPATION is a little handbook of the heart. Honor and respect are the passwords, and the author teaches parents of African descent that culture, as well as charity, begins at home. Brother Vanderhorst calls us back to the African village where the legacy of communal love kept our children sound and safe."

- Dr. Gwedolyn Goldsby Grant, psychologist, advice columnist for ESSENCE MAGAZINE and author of the BEST KIND OF LOVING.

ORDER FORM

Name _____

Address _____

City _____

State _____ Zip Code _____

Quantity _____

Rearing African Children Under American Occupation $7.95 per book. S/H $1.50 + .50 each additional book. Inquire for bulk rates. Allow 2-3 weeks for delivery.

<u>Make checks or money orders payable to:</u> PREPARE OUR YOUTH, INC.

Published by HOTEP PRODUCTIONS
Prepare Our Youth, Inc.
6856 Eastern Avenue NW Suite 207
Washington, D.C. 20012
(202) 291-5040 (202) 291-5042 fax

COMING: SUMMER OF 1997!

WHOLE BRAIN PARENTING

KWAME RONNIE VANDERHORST

Good parenting reviews, revamps and refines interpersonal skills quite often. Good parenting is not static. There is no cruise-control gear in parenting, but good parenting is perpetual forward motion, growth and enhancement.

It is said that humans use only ten percent of our brain. WHOLE BRAIN PARENTING challenges parents to use their 'whole brain' in relationships and parenting.

You may be "a half-a-hemisphere away" from your children (and partner) while living in the same house and never know it unless you read this book!

ORDER FORM

Name _____

Address _____

City _____

State _____ Zip Code _____

Quantity _____

Whole Brain Parenting $9.95 per book. S/H $2.00 + .75 each additional book. Inquire for bulk rates. Allow 2-3 weeks for delivery.

<u>Make checks or money orders payable to:</u> PREPARE OUR YOUTH, INC.

Published by HOTEP PRODUCTIONS
Prepare Our Youth, Inc.
6856 Eastern Avenue NW Suite 207
Washington, D.C. 20012
(202) 291-5040   (202) 291-5042   fax

COMING: SUMMER OF 1997!

EDUCATING AFRICAN CHILDREN UNDER AMERICAN OCCUPATION

KWAME RONNIE VANDERHORST

"There is an educational crisis in African American communities today. For at least a generation, some parents have left the responsibility for the education of our young to a school system that at best is poorly prepared and at worst has little expertise in educating children of African ancestry toward freedom. Education that engenders oppression and dependency is not appropriate to teach liberation. Reclaiming the education of our youth is within our capacity." - Dr. A. Sanford

ORDER FORM

Name _____

Address _____

City _____

State _____ Zip Code _____

Quantity _____

Educating African Children Under American Occupation $8.95 per book. S/H $1.75 + .75 each additional book. Inquire for bulk rates. Allow 2-3 weeks for delivery.

<u>Make checks or money orders payable to:</u> PREPARE OUR YOUTH, INC.

Published by HOTEP PRODUCTIONS
Prepare Our Youth, Inc.
6856 Eastern Avenue NW Suite 207
Washington, D.C. 20012
(202) 291-5040 (202) 291-5042 fax